Simon Garfield is the author of a number of acclaimed books of non-fiction including *A Notable Woman* (as editor), *To the Letter*, *On the Map*, *Just My Type* and *Mauve*. His study of AIDS in Britain, *The End of Innocence*, won the Somerset Maugham Award.

simongarfield.com

'Fascinating and often funny ... What [Garfield] also shows in abundance is the sympathetic understanding of the needs and travails of "ordinary" people that lit up his previous books'
Guardian

'A rare treat, convivial and smart and brimming with intrigue'
Keggie Carew

'If you are someone who appreciates the quirkier byways of human endeavour, there's plenty to surprise and delight in this compendium'
The Times

'Simon Garfield's enthusiasm ... is irresistible'
Spectator

Also by Simon Garfield

Expensive Habits
The End of Innocence
The Wrestling
The Nation's Favourite
Mauve
The Last Journey of William Huskisson
Our Hidden Lives (ed.)
We Are at War (ed.)
Private Battles (ed.)
The Error World
Mini
Exposure
Just My Type
On the Map
To the Letter
My Dear Bessie (ed.)
A Notable Woman (ed.)
Timekeepers

HOW SMALL THINGS
ILLUMINATE THE WORLD

SIMON GARFIELD

CANONGATE

This paperback edition published in Great Britain in 2019 by Canongate
Books

First published in Great Britain in 2018 by Canongate Books Ltd,
14 High Street, Edinburgh EH1 1TE

canongate.co.uk

1

British Library Cataloguing-in-Publication Data
A catalogue record for this book is available on
request from the British Library

ISBN 978 1 78689 079 5

Typeset in Adobe Caslon Pro by Palimpsest Book Production Ltd,
Falkirk, Stirlingshire

Printed and bound in Great Britain by Clays Ltd, Elcograf S.p.A.

For Justine

'By doing something a half centimetre high, you are more likely to get a sense of the universe than if you try to do the whole sky.'

Alberto Giacometti

'The only thing that gets better when it gets bigger is a penis.'

George Lois

Contents

A kingdom at her feet. Princess Elizabeth at Bekonscot Model Village
in the 1930s.

The Art of Seeing

Not so long ago, bigness was the thing. A big pack was better value. The department store had more of everything, as did Texas. *Encyclopaedia Britannica* had all the knowledge and occupied one-sixth of all available living-room shelving.

Then small was beautiful. The toy poodle. The Mini. The boutique. Nouvelle cuisine. The exclusive club. The stacking chair.

And then, in the age of technology, even smaller was all: the microchip, the microwave oven, the in-ear headphone, 1,000 songs in your pocket, the nanosecond, the slider.

A while after that – which brings us to now – things are confusingly big again. The flat-screen television. The Airbus A380. The intractable size of our global economic and security dilemmas. Dwayne Johnson.

Size is one thing, but scale is another, and this book is about scale. It is specifically concerned with how the miniature world informs the world at large. At its heart it is a book about looking, and about seeing; and with this may come elucidation. We bring things down to size to understand and appreciate them. Something too big to visualise at full scale

– a building perhaps, or a war – may be rendered comprehensible at 12:1. Artists – sculptors, set designers, poets – work in miniature because it encourages greater scrutiny and deeper participation, and I hope this book will do the same.

This is also a book about pleasure and vision – a celebration. Miniature items help us imagine grander schemes. A signal box on a model railway is eyed with needling precision, and with the care we would seldom apportion to one at full size. Before we landed on the Moon, at least one NASA scientist clung for inspiration, through difficult times, to the marionettes and rockets on the British television series *Thunderbirds*. Architects of future cities must first scheme in model form, and the model may be the only proof that they attempted such a thing.

Of all the miniature things we'll encounter in the following pages, not all of them will be small. The miniature railway in Hamburg prides itself on being the biggest in the world. The Venetian hotel in Las Vegas, with its fully workable gondola rides for the romantically obtuse, sleeps 4,000. But everything here will be miniature in scale, compared to the thing it's a miniature of.

The word 'miniature' derives from the world of books, but it was popularised by the world of art. Before the printing press, when books were written by scribes and illustrated by hand, the word evolved from the Italian word *miniatura*, which itself derived from the Latin *miniare*, to colour with red lead. There were very few uses of 'miniature' before the sixteenth century, when the word became associated with illumination in general, and became frequently interchangeable with 'limning' or the painting of small portraits. Thereafter, anything small was referred to as miniature, and the word entered common usage from about 1630. The development of both miniature books and miniature portraits will be examined in later chapters, and both will confirm that it is only with close scrutiny that we may uncover secrets within.

To distinguish between the miniature and the merely small I have adopted a simple qualifier: a miniature must be a reduced version of something that was originally bigger, or led to something bigger, and it should be consciously created as such. It may also perform a miniature duty – explain a concept, solve a puzzle, jog a memory. A souvenir of a building on a key ring, though not very interesting, fits the bill. As does a miniature bottle of gin. A Volkswagen Beetle does not, and nor does an ever so small thimble, no matter how keen are those who collect them. Minibars and lapdogs are borderline, as is the art of bonsai cultivation, in which small is created by purposeful pruning and potting. A toy poodle made of plastic in a classroom tableau made by five-year-olds is of no interest to anyone. One could create further rules, and dictate dimensions the way an airline dictates the carry-on, but it will soon become clear that miniatures occupy a significant enough space in our world to create their own instinctual presence: you'll know one if you see one, and after a while you may see nothing else.

The miniature world embraces control. The toys we enjoy

as children invest us with a rare power at a young age, conferring the potency of adults, and possibly giants. Toy cars and dolls and plastic construction kits are not merely pliable in our hands; they render us conquerors. We may never have such dominion over the world again, unless we continue the play into adulthood. Those men with their train driver's caps and their tiny models in sheds and attics! Their wives long gone! And their wives with their own china madnesses, their little toy families, their smooth hedgehog collections, their treasured things in felt. Who will speak for them? The creation of small universes in which we may bury ourselves to the exclusion of all else will be at the core of this book. The people crouching over tiny details as if the world depended on it are only doing it because their world *does* depend on it.

The miniature world is more than an artless conglomeration of miniature things; it is instead a vibrant and deeply rooted ecosystem. The psychology of miniaturisation is an intriguing academic discipline, if a miniature one in itself, hinting at an intricate tangle of connections. The essays in this book are conceived similarly.

The French anthropologist Claude Lévi-Strauss has observed how a miniature may completely reverse the way we comprehend an object: rather than examining it piecemeal and gradually, so that we may slowly derive an understanding of the whole, we see the whole in its entirety and understand it at once – the substitution of what he calls 'sensible dimensions' with 'intelligible dimensions'. This is a humanising force, and it is why we give homey, comical and diminishing names to huge and intrusive structures: those buildings dominating the centre of London nicknamed the Gherkin, Walkie-Talkie and the Cheesegrater – by turns edible and hand-held – are not only fun monikers for us, but also useful for the owners and constructors, transforming what might otherwise be something wholly objectionable and threatening into something instantly friendlier and seemingly smaller.

We would struggle to educate ourselves without models. They have been part of the intellectual architecture of museums for more than 200 years, and it is often the spatial encounter with these objects that make a child's first encounter with a museum memorable. The desire to play with small things becomes a desire to make small things, and both stages address the human need for mastery. We live in a huge and doomy world, and controlling just a tiny scaled-down part of it restores our sense of order and worth. We may not play in the World Cup or the Ryder Cup, but there is always table football and minigolf. What is a drone if not a modern remote-controlled model aeroplane? And what is a globe if not everything we understand about the lay of the land?

I think we may also struggle to educate ourselves without the amateur. The world advances on enthusiasms and ingenuity from the attic and shed (the steam engine, the personal computer), and the miniaturist with the Maplins loyalty card and the early circuit board is almost always an amateur. Until their work is appreciated and valued, they know only private passion and familial disapproval. This book is intended to double our admiration. We should note that the word 'amateur' derives from the Latin word *amare*, to love.

But still: how to explain the model village with a cricket match underway on the village green and the tiny firemen nearby climbing tiny ladders to view the tiny damage to a tiny thatched roof? Who designs and visits these things? What can they tell us about our lives? When Princess Elizabeth stepped among the houses at Bekonscot model village in Buckinghamshire, was she the only visitor that afternoon who believed they ruled the kingdom?

I hardly need add (for you will already have ascertained this from the dimensions of the work) that this is not intended as an encyclopaedia or manual. As well as an introduction to some dedicated people, the book is an attempt to tell the history of a few key events as they've been represented in miniature form, and show how the form informs our deeper comprehension. The wider shores of humanity are thus (and often) explored in ways that would be impossible without this reduction in scale.

We should be grateful that the miniature universe is not policed. It is not created by corporation or committee, but by committed individuals. And in this way the miniature aspires to art: at its best, it may offer up the illuminating and profound. At the very least, it may expand our perception of the things the mind already thinks it knows.

The subject matter dictates that this analysis is a microcosm, and perhaps it's best regarded as a brief history of the model village commonly known as the world. The village is large and welcoming, but it doesn't contain everything. If you are looking for Sylvanian Families or Dinky cars or the history of Lego you will be disappointed, but if you are in the market for a flea circus, 1,000 tiny Hitlers and the revolving model box used by the set designer of *Angels in America*, then you're in luck.

Almost all the miniature objects here have been made by hand. These days, such objects – a miniature book, an elaborate model train layout, the luminescent portrait on ivory – would be considered part of the maker movement, or perhaps the slow movement. Often they are things out of time – not always nostalgic, but frequently redolent of childhood, or the myth of childhood. And of course we will enter the arena of the obsessive, and wonder if there has ever been a more desirable place to be.

The powerful kingdoms of fantasy and Hollywood lie beyond our village borders, so there is only fleeting reference to *Gulliver's Travels* and hardly any space at all for shrinking portal transportations or the movie *Downsizing*. (A flea circus is included not because it involves fleas – I'm not interested in small things per se, and even less in things created small in the natural world – but because it is a minuscule circus. The fleas try to do things that exist in the human world – they dance a ballet, fight a duel with swords, drive a mail van; they are a wonder to us. The training of circus fleas has its own academic specialism: 'pulicology'. Reader, try putting this book back on the shelf *now* . . .)

The significance of the miniature is not new, and neither

is it slight, which makes the paucity of writing on its collective value a mystery, at least to me. The desire for the miniature that begins in childhood is usually jettisoned as adulthood approaches, the way the boosters fall off as the rocket streaks towards the Moon: teenagers don't want toy cars, they want real cars. And if they don't, they may be considered peculiar, and it is this peculiarity that captivates us. Before I entered the miniature world, I regarded with suspicion the sign on the door of the doll's house emporium near my home that says 'this is not a toy shop'. For what else could it be? But when I gathered the courage to enter (the shop is dark, imposing and sits behind mesh grilles, and the owner has a reputation), I found tiny tennis racquets with real stringing, and jars of Marmite so small that even a mouse wouldn't be satisfied come teatime, and hundreds of other tiny things too familiar to mention. It wasn't a toy shop, it was a universe. It performed that familiar miniature trick: it had indelible belief in its own existence. And because everything was miniature, nothing looked small. I left the shop believing that the cars outside were juggernauts, and the pillar box was the size of the Guggenheim.

Worlds within worlds existed long before those suggested by Lewis Carroll or quantum physics. The history of the miniature stretches back to the ancients, and its path tracks an irreducible line. Lucretius had it right when he observed, 'A small thing may give an analogy of great things, and show the tracks of knowledge.' In her book *On Longing*, the poet Susan Stewart suggests that we inhabit a daydream in which the world of the miniature may one day reveal a secret life. The daydream maintains an internal logic: as we fall down the rabbit hole, we should instantly forgive anyone who considers the larger everyday world to be the normal one.

The following chapters will, I hope, both celebrate and clarify our fascination with bringing things down to size in order to grasp their essence. Very shortly, Egyptian pharaohs, English abolitionists and Rod Stewart will all have their say, as will a woman from Chicago who believes the only way to solve a crime is to reduce it to its smallest constituent parts. But the story begins on a grand scale 130 years ago in the centre of Paris, where Gustave Eiffel is ascending his tower in a stiff wind, and the excitements of human engineering are changing for all time the way we view the world.

'Like some fabled city descending to the bottom of the sea': the view of
maintenance workers on the Eiffel Tower in 1924.

Chapter One

The View from Above

Amid the many expressions of outrage and delight that accompanied the opening of the Eiffel Tower in the late spring of 1889, there was one response that took even its creators by surprise. Visitors were shocked to find that the tallest structure on earth had suddenly shrunk the world around it.

Anyone possessed of the immense courage necessary to climb the 363 steps to the first platform, and then 381 to the second, saw the world beneath anew. A cliché now, but then it was a revelation: people had become ants. This is what the birth of modernism looked like: an iron-clad sense of upward progress coupled with an omniscient sense of measured order. From above, Paris was both map and metaphor. Unless you had previously floated in a balloon, this was the first time the world appeared to scale: Haussmann's boulevards became grids; the World's Fair glittered like a bauble below, and its chaos was momentarily quelled. The thrill of the climb culminated in blissful serenity: the stench of horse manure and soot just evaporated. On a clear day the views stretched to Fontainebleau and Normandy, to the chalk of Dover and the inglorious Belgian battlefields of Waterloo, and, beyond that, to the clear pure future of everything.

Because all of this was new, it was also noteworthy. Those who went up the Eiffel Tower in the first few months kept a careful record of what they saw, for their way of seeing was as new as the tower itself. Reading their prose today, we may still perceive their wonder humming along the gantries. 'He climbs slowly, with his right hand on the bannister,' one reporter noted as he followed Gustave Eiffel up the stairs before the official opening (even the climbing was novel; the highest fixed view before had been the gallery at Notre Dame). 'He swings his body from one hip to the other, using the momentum of the swing to negotiate each step.' Even on the first platform (190 feet) 'the city already appears immobile. The silhouettes of passers-by and fiacres are like little black spots of ink in the streets.' The ascension continues until, at 900 feet, 'Paris seems to be sinking into the night like some fabled city descending to the bottom of the sea amid a murmur of men and church bells.' A few weeks later, once the tower had opened to the public, another observer described how '975 feet above the world people become pigmies . . . all that looked large had disappeared'. Eiffel himself described it as 'soul-inspiring' and hinted at the possibility of achieving a form of transcendence hitherto impossible – a higher, weightless plane. A reporter from *Le Temps* found he was overtaken by 'an indescribable melancholy, a feeling of intellectual prostration . . .' At 350 feet, 'the earth is still a human spectacle; an ordinary scale of comparisons is still adequate to make sense of it. But at 1,000 feet I felt completely beyond the normal conditions of experience.' The art critic Robert Hughes has observed that for the vast numbers who ascended the tower in its first few months the view 'was as significant in 1889 as the sight of the Earth from the Moon would be 80 years later'.

The view from above continues to enthral: the thrill from the Shard or the Empire State is, at first sight, quite as enticing as the one that transfixed Parisians in 1889. Thirty years after the tower opened, the writer Violet Trefusis experienced the same thrill in an aeroplane. She called herself a 'puny atom', and she felt her old self die. She saw 'a little map dotted with little towns, and a little sea', and thought 'what a wretched little place the world is! Humanity had been wiped out . . . It seemed to me that I had become suddenly and miraculously purged of all meanness, all smallness of spirit, all deceit.' That peculiar combination of humility and awe – how insignificant we are among the clouds, but how significant to have advanced towards them – does not change with the seasons or the admission prices; they are adventures in scale, and in seeing our world afresh. Eiffel had given us 1,000 feet, the early plane 3,000; from all heights, the view beneath was miniature and the city beneath was ours.

Eiffel had designed his tower as a symbol of formal strength, a *tour de force*, the triumph of the machine astride a city hitherto fondly regarded for tender aesthetics. Its dizzying height was its virtue and its point. It was symbolism without purpose, and no wonder so many literary lights took against it. No one did so more vociferously than Guy de Maupassant, who classified it as 'an ever-present and racking nightmare'. His loathing only intensified after it opened: the fable goes that, before he fled Paris to avoid the tower, he felt compelled to patronise one of the tower's second-platform restaurants, for it was the only place in Paris he was in no danger of seeing the tower itself. Maupassant was joined in his indignation by fellow writer Léon Bloy, who tagged it a 'truly tragic lamp post'.

But the public loved it, of course, and we still do. In the first week, almost 30,000 paid 40 centimes to climb to the first level, while 17,000 paid 20 centimes more to go to the second. Almost two million ventured at least part of the way during its starring role at the Exposition Universelle between May and October 1889, and many were delighted to encounter M. Eiffel himself, installed in his office halfway up. Here he welcomed Thomas Edison, Buffalo Bill, Annie Oakley, Grand Duke Vladimir of Russia, King George of Greece and the Prince of Wales.

But what use was the tower beyond scaling down the world beneath it? Its creator, troubled by the thought that others might see it as inconsequential and hubristic – a toy even – worked hard to establish its worth. (It's fair to say that its investors had no such qualms – in its first five months the tower took admission fees of almost six million francs.) But Eiffel had aims beyond avarice, and inscribed the names of more than seventy

French scientists around the first level to justify his monument, and perhaps equate his accomplishment with theirs. He stressed that his tower would have many meteorological and astronomical applications, and might even serve an important role in defence, should Paris ever come under attack.

But above all, and at its heart, the Eiffel Tower *was* a toy, and the lifts also made it a ride, and everyone could have a turn on it. It was a plaything for the newly wealthy industrialist, and it was a grand day out for *tout le monde*. The public needed none of the scientific justification sought by its engineer; they loved it merely for its wonder.

But something else began at the Eiffel Tower: the ability, at the end of the day, to take it home. The opening of the tower marked the birth of the mass-consumed souvenir and the dawn of the factory-made scale model. The Shah of Persia left with a tower-topped walking cane and two dozen iron miniatures, enough for the whole harem. Other visitors found trinkets at every turn, with kiosks on every floor. Predictably, Guy de Maupassant didn't like this either: not only was the tower visible from every point in the city, 'but it could be found everywhere, made of every kind of known material, exhibited in all windows . . .' The Eiffel Tower not only shrunk the world, but it shrunk the world on your mantelpiece too. Henceforth, a symbol only truly became part of the landscape when it also became part of one's luggage home.

The tower was available in pastry and chocolate. Handkerchiefs, tablecloths, napkin rings, candlesticks, inkstands, watch chains – if something could be made tall, triangular and pointy it was. The most dazzling was the *Tour en diamants*, 40,000 stones in all, on show at the Galerie Georges Petit in the tower's shadow. But the tower was also available in less precious metals in every other shop, and almost 130 years later production has yet to slow. Gustave Eiffel believed that souvenir rights were his to trade, and he granted an exclusive image licence to the Printemps department store on Boulevard Haussmann. The agreement lasted but a few days, or just until every other Parisian shopkeeper brought a class action lawsuit arguing that such a magnificent day out in the sky should be celebrated and exploited by all.

The word 'souvenir' is, naturally, French. Its translation denotes its purpose: 'to remember' (an earlier version of the word first appears in Latin: *subvenire* – to bring to mind). A miniature souvenir does not diminish its worth, for its partiality supplies its force: it provokes a longing to remember and tell its story. The Eiffel Tower at sunset, drink in hand, just the two of you, we'll always have Paris – that's never a story that gets any smaller.

Of course, true miniaturists may not be content until they have made the souvenir themselves. Frequently in these pages we will encounter miniaturisation as an all-consuming hobby, and we will discover that our appetite to manipulate a reduced world is only partially sated by ownership; we also must satisfy our innate human need to create. A handmade miniature Eiffel Tower was always going to be a challenge, but the ultimate challenge would be to make it out of something that was both seemingly impossible and evidently stupid. So we should, in the first instance, admire both the application and the triumph of a New York dental student who, in 1925, built a model of the tower with 11,000 toothpicks. According to *Popular Mechanics*, which photographed the student in a long white coat 'putting finishing touches' to the model just a little taller than he was, the whole enterprise required tweezers, glue and approximately 300 hours. And there was a scientific justification for it: by building the model from toothpicks, the unnamed student confirmed the triangular structural rigidity of the genuine tower (not that this really needed proving after so many millions had ascended it).

In the 1950s, a 5-foot version was made in Buenos Aires, this time from international toothpicks gathered from all over the world: a global media appeal yielded an enthusiastic response from hundreds, and they mailed in their wooden splinters as if reacting to an emergency disaster appeal. After that it was only a matter of time before the enthusiast's material of choice switched from toothpicks to matchsticks, and so it proved when a Detroit man named Howard Porter occupied his days by gluing together an Eiffel model at 1:250th scale using 1,080 small matches, 110 larger fireplace matches, and, for old times' sake, 1,200 toothpicks. Like the model by the New York student, this also took around 300 hours to build, but both of them would be made to look like lightweights compared to the French watchmaker Georges Vitel and family, who spent several years and an estimated half a million matchsticks building the tower at 1:10th scale. When the French press celebrated it in 1961 (*'La Tour Eiffel – En Allumettes!'*) it was almost big enough to climb. Better

Seventy kilos of matchsticks: the Vitel family applying the finishing touches in their living room.

still, or worse still, the 70-kilo model was wired up to the mains. The electrics operated the internal lifts, and lit the lamps in the tower's restaurants. Because Georges Vitel and his family didn't live in a chateau, but in a quiet suburban house in Grigny, almost 30 kilometres south of Paris, the team had to build the model in two sections, top and bottom, both of which reached the ceiling of their living room. They had a television, but the tower blocked the view. Was this part of a life well spent, or was there a suggestion that the Vitels judged life so disappointing that all that remained for them to do was bolt the doors and get matchsticking?

A miniature, even a miniature that reaches the ceiling, is a souvenir in physical form, a commemoration of our own tiny imprint on the planet. We made this, we say; we bought this. We understand and appreciate this. Sometimes we control this. These are fundamental human desires, and they lie at the heart of our lives and at the heart of this book. But what happens when we believe that a miniature souvenir from this world may be carried forward to the next?

Séthi Iᵉʳ
1294-1279 av. J.-C. (19ᵉ dynastie)
faïence siliceuse   E 4884, N 2248, N 466

Safe passage to the underworld, and an afterlife of leisure: shabtis from
the tomb of Seti I in the Louvre.

Mini-break, 3000 BCE:
Egypt's Coffins

On 16 October 1817, the great Italian Egyptologist Giovanni Battista Belzoni instructed his workers to start digging at the foot of a steep hill in the Valley of the Kings on the west bank of the Nile. His diggers were dubious: why would there be anything at all in this waterlogged place? (It was more than a century before the tomb of Tutankhamun was discovered nearby.) Towards the end of the following day, 18 feet down, Belzoni's workers hit rock. The rock was the entrance to the tomb of King Seti I, the ruling pharaoh of Egypt for more than a decade before his death in 1279 BCE. The tomb was elaborate and well preserved, and within it lay evidence of how we once invested the miniature with profound responsibility.

Signor Belzoni, a high-collared dandy who was as much at home in the temples of high fashion as he was in crumbling mummy pits, loved astonishing audiences with his tomb-raiding adventures (in London, in earlier and more downtrodden days, he developed his showmanship as a strongman in a circus). He once wrote of a Theban discovery where his face made contact with decaying Egyptian mummies as he passed by, and where he 'could not avoid being covered with bones, legs, arms and heads rolling from above.' He described walking the deep chambers beneath the Valley of the Kings with equal drama, of encountering deep wells and hidden side rooms with hieroglyphics and paintings that looked as if they had been created yesterday (there were ten chambers off seven corridors). He tunnelled his way into great pillared halls and found staircases that led to chambers he named the Room of Beauties (paintings of women on the wall), the Bull's Room (containing a mummified bull) and the Room of Mysteries (no one knows). He found wooden statues and papyrus rolls, and as he went further and deeper he came to the final burial chamber holding an ornately carved alabaster sarcophagus. 'It is useless to proceed any further in the description of this heavenly place,' he wrote, 'as I can assure the reader he can form but a very faint idea of it from the trifling account my pen is able to give; should I be so fortunate, however, as to succeed in erecting an exact model of this tomb in Europe, the beholder will acknowledge the impossibility of doing it justice in a description.'

In 1821 Belzoni did manage to bring a few of his discoveries to London's Piccadilly, and they attracted a large public. Alongside other treasures, Belzoni brought several intricately carved figurines made from blue-glazed pottery that had been buried with King Seti's body. These were shabti dolls, between 7 and 9 inches tall, each with a symbolic role to play in the Egyptian vision of what happened after death. Each would relieve the travelling soul from performing manual work in the afterlife, the precise nature of the task revealed in the hands crossed against the shabti's chest: a vase may release the bearer from serving or vineyard work, while a basket would rule out harvest or other reaping chores. While those buried around 2000 BCE might have been accompanied to the next world by only one or two shabtis, the wealthier souls of Egypt living in the later dynasties between 300 and 30 BCE would be buried with several hundred. For a while the tradition became 401: one worker for every day of the year, and a string of 'overseers' holding whips to keep the workers in line.

The shabti is far from the oldest miniature representation of the human form. This accolade belongs to Venus figurines, usually obese and naked, and just a few centimetres tall, that date back 40,000 years. Only about 200 of these plump carvings are known to exist, whereas there are tens of thousands of later shabtis (which are also known as ushabtis and shawabties, depending on place of origin). The shabtis were made from limestone, granite, alabaster, clay, wood, bronze and glass, but most commonly from the blue-green sand-based pottery known as faience.

Because of their ubiquity, shabtis may be seen performing all manner of funereal tasks in Egyptology departments throughout the world. The Egyptian Museum in Cairo holds more than 40,000. Some of the finest examples are to be found in institutions in north-west England, including museums in Rochdale, Stockport, Macclesfield and Warrington, many of the exhibits gathered from the private collections and the

'cabinets of curiosities' of industrialists and gentlemen archaeologists of the nineteenth century. The British Museum also
has a great hoard, including the magnificently preserved figu-
rine of King Seti I, one of the shabtis discovered by Giovanni
Belzoni 200 years ago, resembling a miniature mummy with
a striped royal headdress. The figure carries two implements,
a hoe and a mattock (an ancient pickaxe), and is inscribed
with a passage from the Book of the Dead, the collection of
spells that ensured a safe passage through the underworld.

It's uncertain whether Belzoni secured his own passage to
the afterlife, but at least his legacy is secure. He died in
Nigeria in 1823 from either a) dysentery or b) being murdered,
but the Theban world he uncovered in 1817 is still being
explored, and almost every year there are exciting new finds.
In 2016 a team from the Polish Centre of Mediterranean
Archaeology working near Luxor discovered a hoard of shabtis
in a hitherto unexplored burial site in a nameless hillock.
More than 1,000 fragments were found, from which 647
statues were formed. Thirteen distinct types were identified
– the majority in mud, clay or alabaster – and although there
were both workers and overseers, none could be linked to an
owner. They were simple figures, most of them inexact and
indecipherable, ranging from approximately 2 to 5 inches tall.
Many looked as though they were designed in a great hurry.
Some of them were no more than pegs.

The archaeologists wondered whether finer examples had
previously been removed by grave robbers. What remained
were predominantly good-luck charms for the well-connected

commoner, each carrying two or three rough-hewn spells into the unknown. The lack of definition in the figures, and their paucity in number for each owner, revealed a familiar logic: even in miniature, even 3,000 years ago, there was one after-life for the rich and quite another for the poor. But everyone seemed to believe that, contrary to received wisdom, you could indeed take something with you.

A melon cauli world: Bekonscot Model Village displays
its painful wares.

Chapter Two

Miniature Villages and Cities, Some Happier than Others

On Wednesday, 27 May 1925, a newspaper reporter from the *Kansas City Star* named Landon Laird arrived in Springfield, Missouri, on special assignment. Another reporter named H. Niemeyer of the *St Louis Post-Dispatch* was on his way to join him. What was the fuss? The fuss was a model village called Tiny Town, situated at Grant Beach Park, by then in its third day and attracting unprecedented crowds. Those who attended said they had never seen anything like it before, and that was because there had never been anything like it before – not in Missouri, and not anywhere.

Tiny Town consisted of about 1,200 buildings and all the civic amenities one would expect in a modern urban development. Houses were made from wood, brick and concrete, and ranged from bungalows to palatial colonial residences. There was a town hall, several schools, a library with miniature books, fully equipped playgrounds and many churches. The interiors of all dwellings were properly decorated, and most had electricity. There was a business district and several residential areas, and local road contractors were employed to secure the surfaces against inclement weather. Because it was 1925, and Tiny Town was forward-thinking, stables were out and garages were in, and many houses had little cars in the drive. A week before it opened to the public, the *Springfield Missouri Republican* noted that the town would soon have lakes with glistening water, and 'all kinds of foliage to represent shade trees, and well-placed shrubbery will edge the avenues and adorn the lawns'. The scale was one inch to the foot, and occupied an area of 250 feet by 1,000 feet.

The town had been built by children from schools all over Springfield, and the big idea was to teach civic governance, so kids ran the place too. School elections had seen a 98 per cent turnout, and keen students Naomi Sherwood, Daise Eaton and Margaret Bradshaw had, against all gender practices in the adult world, been appointed to the posts of Municipal Judge, Commissioner of Recreation and Commissioner of City Planning. This was surely the way of the future! But the future lasted only until the following Sunday, when the *Springfield Missouri Republican* reported business as usual: 'The boys built the houses and garages and churches and power plants' while 'the girls drew plans for all kinds of residences, planned interiors, made color schemes, fitted and hung the draperies.'

Tiny Town was due to last for two weeks, from 25 May to 6 June, but it had been such a hit that the kids voted to keep it open for another week. Visitors first read about the extension in *Tiny Town Times*, the daily newspaper composed on site. Despite its name, all the newspapers called Tiny Town a city. Everyone marvelled at it – a delightful plan perfectly executed. It certainly made a nice contrast to the last time the big newspapers had been to Springfield almost twenty years before, to cover a lynching.

Tiny Town was the commercial idea of William H. Johnson, a Springfield real estate agent. Admission was 25 cents for adults and 10 cents for children, and that would cover the costs of construction. But the real boost was to the full-size building trade. Johnson had noted a slump in new development, and had suggested to the chamber of commerce that even a modest sponsored upturn would generate enough confidence and momentum to encourage new homebuyers. If this wasn't possible on a grand scale, then they could try a smaller one. 'If schoolboys can be induced to build some miniature houses, the building microbe may attack the parents of those boys.' An advertisement in the papers certainly caught the bug: 'The little folks are building houses,' observed the Burton Building and Loan Association. 'Why not build yourself a home? Don't dream alone – realize!'

And after three weeks it was over. There is no reliable evidence as to how the local building industry fared as a result of Tiny Town, or how those who were encouraged to buy new mortgages coped in the ensuing depression. But the exposition certainly put Springfield on the map. The US has many Springfields, but for a miniature moment the one in Missouri shone as brightly as the one that would later contend with Bart Simpson. And the ensuing publicity may have had a positive effect on population growth: from 1920 to 1930 it increased by 45 per cent to 57,500. Most of the model houses were destroyed, and the land flattened again, though a few models won prizes for their makers and were placed in the city's shop windows. During its three-week run, Tiny Town reported no crime and no drunken behaviour. It was a clean, efficiently run city, and the young people who made it could be forgiven for feeling nostalgic as they grew into adults.

In November 2017, on the way back from another model village, three children between the ages of eight and ten were discussing what they liked best. Nikolaos said that he thought there would have been lots of plasticky things, but it was much more varied than that. Athina said she thought she'd be able to lift up the buildings and see every detail inside, like a doll's house, and that it would be more like Lego and more childish. They all liked the canal, and Kanak liked the house with the pottery inside, and the tiny circus where the figures did tricks with horses. If they had been able to shrink themselves into a scene then that circus would have been a good place to sit, as would one of the moving sailboats on the canal. They all liked the church with the ringing bells, and the railway that stopped regularly at stations. The children, two of whom were my neighbours, said that if they lived in that model their lives would be quite safe and there would be a lot of open air and sporting activity. Athina, who is smaller than some of her classmates, said that she felt as though she ruled the place.

The village, which was in Beaconsfield in Buckinghamshire, prime London commuter belt, was called Bekonscot, and, unlike Tiny Town in Springfield, it was still going. In fact, Bekonscot was coming up to its ninetieth birthday. Nikolaos said as we drove home: 'It's not like everyday life. You wouldn't travel forty-five minutes from London to see something that you could see in London. You would only travel forty-five minutes if it was something special.'

More than sixty years before, Enid Blyton had written of her own visit to Bekonscot in an account entitled 'The Enchanted Village'. She'd fallen for the place like everyone else. 'Would you like to come with me and visit a village so small that you will tower above the houses?' she asked her readers. 'Well I live quite near to a little village like this – it is so close that I can see it from my bedroom window.' Blyton had moved with her family to Beaconsfield in 1938, at the age of forty, the war looming. There was no threat of war at Bekonscot, and when it was over there were no signs that there had ever been one. Blyton's story was published with photographs of two children named John and Mary towering over things, and as she marvels at what she sees, Blyton becomes a child again herself. 'It's a real village,' she writes. 'We see the old village houses – their roofs are hardly up to my waist! We look at the tiny tiles on the roof, and the little bricks in the wall – yes, all built by hand. What a magical place!' And then John sees the miniature railway that runs throughout. 'Look,' he says, struck with delight. 'LOOK!'

A visitor to Bekonscot today may believe that little has changed for ninety years. We become what the writer Ally Ireson calls 'mesmerised literalists'. We walk around very slowly, and we point things out to our children as if they didn't have eyes themselves. There are clothes on washing lines in back gardens. There is a cricket match on the green. There is smoke coming from a thatched roof, but the firemen are on hand. At the racecourse, a policeman chases a ne'er-do-well across a field. Another man is being chased by a bull. Gravediggers are digging in the cemetery. The names of shops are terrible: the bookshop is 'Ann Ecdote', the butcher is 'Sam and Ella'; you point them out with glee and smugness, but you slink away in embarrassment (the greengrocer is called 'Chris P. Lettis'). Everything appears to be happening for the visitor at that very moment, as if, in this otherwise staid and well-mannered environment, we have stumbled upon a whole year's worth of excitement within our ninety-minute visit. We don't just observe a chimpanzee's tea party at the zoo, but a tea party where a chimp has chucked food over his head.

The figures are hand-carved from lime wood or moulded in resin. There is an agreeable amateurishness about them, and they are not without a point of view. The caricatures are keen: many of the women have huge busts; many of the men look like bores. There is 7,000 feet of railway track incorporating 22,000 sleepers; there are 6,000 metres of subterranean electrical cable powering the trains and house lights and boats in the lake. There are 8,000 conifers, and every few years when they grow too big and can't be convincingly manicured they are replaced by smaller ones. The total area measures about 40,000 square feet. Nearing the close of 2017, more than 15.4 million people had visited since it opened, which is greater than the population of Greece or Portugal; for several days after Princess Elizabeth, the future Queen, visited at the age of seven in 1933, many thousands who had queued for admission had to be turned away. The scale of the railway is 1:32, while the model village is predominantly 1:12 to 1:18, and most visitors either don't notice or don't care. For this is the 1930s, and all is as it should be. Inevitably, and gratefully, visitors are rewarded with an ice cream at the end of it.

But things *have* changed. It is not really the 1930s we see, but a vision of what we hope the 1930s were like – those mythical last great summers before the skies filled with Lancasters. These are not all original stone and wooden buildings; some have been made to look old, but were made in the 1970s and 1980s. For several decades, Bekonscot tried to keep pace with modern life; there were some brutalist constructions placed amongst the mock-Tudor semis, and diesel railways replaced steam, and on the airfield modern jets (including Concorde) made an appearance. New adverts for the latest and swingiest products began to appear alongside older ones for Colman's Mustard. But then, with the pace of life accelerating, and the historical integrity of Bekonscot looking increasingly confusing, the village elders decided that the model should go back to its roots. So the modern world was banished, or at least repainted. The 1930s were just recreated: a modern town hall became a posh private residence, and the pylons and concrete slabs of modernism were disappeared.

But even then there were difficult questions of attribution and provenance. No one could say for sure just how the village came to be, or what its founder intended. The most satisfying story begins with a housebound miniature railway that grew so big that a wife reached for the rolling pin: either it went or she did. The husband, a man named Roland Robert Callingham, a successful accountant, found a third way, and in 1927 went outside to colonise the garden. The village grew around the railway, but soon became an obsession: after the standard railway buildings there was suddenly a castle and a church and miniature lawns, followed by the shops and the population to inhabit them. Callingham did some construction himself, and had much assistance from his gardener and local modellers. But it was a private pastime, and it only became an attraction when friends of the Callinghams, who arrived to play tennis or swim, suggested that on occasional weekends the public should be allowed in too. And so Bekonscot opened to all in 1931, and what was a quaint local novelty attracted national press coverage and then royalty; early visitors reported occasional public sightings of its owner still dipping in the pool. Its name was a composite of Beaconsfield and Ascot, the latter the home of the man in charge of the trains. Soon the whole place was a composite: the train station Maryloo sprung from Marylebone and Waterloo; the architecture drew inspiration from quaint suburbia and urban grandeur, from architects George Gilbert Scott, Edwin Lutyens and Berthold Lubetkin. Many of the half timbered structures reflected the aspirations of its owners, a nostalgia for finer things even in the 1930s, something architectural historian Osbert Lancaster called 'Wimbledon Transitional'. One day a miniature version of Enid Blyton's own mock-Tudor house appeared on the lawns.

As ever within a miniature landscape, those who look closer are rewarded with something more, in this case something darker. Most come to Bekonscot for containment and trimmed privets, for a place forever amber. But the rough-hewn figures also suggest unease. Base human emotions don't tend to change much from one era to another, or from one scale to another, and so even in miniature it is possible to detect cattiness in the pub gossip, and a twitching of the curtains, and we may speculate whether a certain blankness in the gaze of many hundreds of the figurines (there are about 3,000 in all) isn't a result of stupefying tedium; if they could, would they ask us to spring them free? When the *World of Interiors* visited in 2007, it photographed a stark row of topless male sunbathers on loungers, with one of them fallen and facing down submissively onto stone. Bekonscot, the magazine concluded with uncharacteristic anxiety, is possessed with a 'special strangeness'. Viewed at an angle, the 1930s may indeed resemble a claustrophobic and deceptive decade. What was the Bekonscot butcher stamping on? Who was being buried, and could we possibly intervene before a bride married a man with red lips and a cold, pinched stare? As Auden had it, 'Who can live for long / In an euphoric dream'?

It was only a matter of time before Bekonscot received an Enid Blyton reboot. This arrived in 1992, when the writer Will Self, who had been fascinated by miniature worlds since reading Lewis Carroll and Jonathan Swift as a child, published a short story entitled 'Scale'. It concerned many things, and it weighed in with all the peacock erudition one has come to expect from the author. 'Scale' played on scale: scale in a kettle, scales on a lizard, everything but musical notation. The narrator of the story, a morphine addict and connoisseur of dystopian motorway systems, is recently divorced, the result of an experience with the family au pair on a set of bathroom . . . scales.

So the narrator moves out of the big family house, and ends up living in a bungalow near Bekonscot. In fact, he is so near to the model village that he is able to claim, when the council calculates his rates, that his dwelling is in fact part of the attraction itself, and is therefore liable to an annual rateable charge of only £11.59. The village also invades his dreams. In one sequence he imagines himself within the grounds, peering in through the window of a tiny art gallery. The gallery is displaying netsuke the narrator has carved himself – miniature representations of extant pieces by the sculptor Anthony Caro. Spying his own bungalow within the grounds, he finds himself reduced in size and happily able to fit inside. Then he shrinks yet smaller, and is able to roam the bungalow within the bungalow, and so on through six stages of shrinkage, at one point positioning himself on a sun porch 'for which a double-glazing estimate would have to be calculated in angstroms'. He is only able to escape wasps the size of zeppelins and the terrifying giant that is a Bekonscot maintenance man by using a rope plaited from strands of carpet underlay. (Self's fantasy reminded me of a short story by Hermann Hesse published during the Second World War in the resistance periodical *Fontaine*. Hesse imagines a prisoner painting a picture on the wall of his cell, an image of a train entering a tunnel. As his gaoler comes for him, the prisoner makes himself tiny and climbs aboard the train in an effort to escape. Heroically he succeeds, and as he does so, smoke appears in the tunnel, 'then this smoke blew away, and with it the picture, and with the picture my person'.)

Like Self, we are drawn to the apparent integrity of the Bekonscot vision. And instead of helping the tiny wooden figures to escape, sometimes we just want in. Look at that cricket pitch, for example: it's probably a Sunday, and, judging from the kit, the sun's out. A hopeful fielder runs to catch a ball in mid-air. He's looking up, both expectant and anxious, aware that in the next moment he will become either hero or schmuck; for now, forever poised perilously between the two, he's just like us. Perhaps only a true work of art could withstand this level of scrutiny for almost a century. At the moment Bekonscot looks like the full English Brexit: idyllic in its imagination, disillusioned in its present, unfathomable to the outside world. And not all is quite what it seems. In a decade or three it might once again look like bliss.

There are many other model villages, of course. In the holiday Britain of the early 1960s it was difficult not to trip over one en route to the minigolf. But then the Costa del Sol and the permissive society arrived, and miniature innocence went the way of the girdle and the Teasmade. Occasionally the dream of the miniature village was resurrected, but the love was gone. Those who have visited Tucktonia in Dorset (1976–86), for example, may recall its large-scale recreation of Hadrian's Wall, Windsor Castle and several famous spots in London (Big Ben about twice the size of an adult, the GPO Tower twice as big again). But the place looked fake without any redeeming features – partly, one imagines, because it wasn't crafted with patience and exasperation through many decades by damp volunteers, but the opposite: it was a bald commercial enterprise thrown up in eighteen months to accompany amusement park rides. Tucktonia was opened by Arthur Askey, and lasted ten years. It must have been truly dreadful in the rain. With the exception of Buckingham Palace, all the sad structures were either crushed, chopped or burned in a barn fire.

Among those villages still standing and cared for are Bourton-on-the-Water in Gloucestershire (an accurate copy of the town at 1:9 scale that 'enables our American cousins to see Bourton-on-the-Water nine times more quickly'). There is Snowshill Manor in the same county (based on one of the very earliest model villages in Hampstead, London, but now resettled near Stow-on-the-Wold, where it more closely resembles a Cornish fishing cove); Babbacombe in Torquay (featuring, in inexplicably close proximity, Stonehenge and the Shard); and Godshill on the Isle of Wight, which has a model village in its model village of the model village, the latter scaled down to 1:1,000.

Miniature villages are disproportionately a British obsession (not least, perhaps, because centuries before Brexit the British Isles had already been a proud, isolated village within the world). But the rest of the world boasts model villages too. In the United States, nothing has bettered Springfield's Tiny Town from 1925, but one can only have a soft spot for Tiny Town, Colorado, which is still going almost a century after its birth in 1920, and this despite some terrible calamities. You'll find them all on its website:

> 1929 – Flood damages Tiny Town.
> 1932 – Another flood damages Tiny Town.
> 1935 – A disastrous fire destroys the Indian pueblo and all the principal buildings of Tiny Town . . .
> 1969 – A disastrous flood destroys Tiny Town . . .
> 1977 – Lyle Fulkerson is killed by a runaway train car on his way to Tiny Town.
> 1978 – Tiny Town closes and falls into disrepair.

But Tiny Town has weathered these awful fates and been resurrected, so hooray for Tiny Town.

And we ignore at our peril the indoor delights of Roadside America in Shartlesville, Pennsylvania, which includes 6,000 square feet of model railroad, a coal mine, a Wild West show-down (pretty much obligatory), push-button mechanisations (ditto) and hokey panoramic projections (ditto). It opened in 1935 and hasn't changed since the early 1960s, but the best feature of Roadside America is its birthing story. Its founder L.T. Gieringer claimed that when he was a child he believed that the faraway Highland Hotel on Neversink Mountain (a real place) was merely a toy waiting to be plucked off the mountain at will, only to find it was a fully functioning and unpluckable hotel when he got closer. And so he created his miniature dreams in his later years, and they are yet to disappoint. (At this juncture, some readers may be reminded of an episode of *Father Ted* in which, with the aid of toy cows and a glance towards a rural scene with real cows, Ted explains to Dougal the significant difference between small and far away.)

Never to be outdone by mythical America, a major miniature world in Shenzhen has magnificence built into its name: Splendid China. This showcases the Terracotta Warriors and the Three Gorges Dam, and claims in its promotional material to permit visitors to see all of China's highlights in a day (this is clearly one thing a lot of these villages have in common, no matter where they are in the world: the ability to see all the sights without actually seeing even one). Splendid China contains 25 replica villages and 50,000 tiny clay figures. The place was such a success that it inspired worldwide franchising. When they opened a Splendid China in Florida in 1993, at a reported cost of $100m, it drew curious crowds eager to see the half-mile Great Wall and a special show featuring authentic full size acrobats from the People's Republic. But it then became distinctly unsplendid: many of the acrobats defected, and there were newspaper stories about Communist propaganda efforts in the village's Mongolian and Tibetan sections. The attraction closed in 2003, and, following widespread looting and rat infestation, the site was earmarked to become a Margaritaville Resort, named after the strung-out song by Jimmy Buffet.

Back in Europe, one could quite feasibly spend a fortnight ankle-deep in resin and polyurethane as the world shrinks within walled borders. We could begin at Madurodam in The Hague, a commendable and charitable institution since 1952, inspired by Bekonscot and featuring everything you wanted to know about Dutch buildings and history at a scale of 1:25 (this is the norm for walk-around miniature parks: model people come up to your heels, bungalows up to your ankles and the Eiffel Tower looms overhead at 12 metres). And then we could hop over to Catalunya en Miniatura near Barcelona, a relatively new addition to the collection (1983), a tribute to the dazzling confectionery of Antoni Gaudí and more than 130 other, flatter Catalonian structures including the home of FC Barcelona, Camp Nou, and a miniature of the Dalí museum, Torre Galatea. And from there it's surely just a leap away to Minimundus in Carinthia, Austria, another incongruous global aggregation of the White House and the Taj Mahal, and then just one leap more to France Miniature, in Élancourt, where the Eiffel Tower finally feels at home.

The cutest of all is undoubtedly Swissminiatur on the banks of Lake Lugano. In the 1970s, when the exchange rate worked in their favour, this was the most popular tourist attraction in Switzerland for Italians. They hopped over the border with lire that would buy the cheapest booze and fags, and, deciding to make a full day of it, then spent many happy hours teetering over the monument to William Tell and an intricately crafted Alpine cheese dairy. These days Swissminiatur struggles to be the most popular tourist attraction even in the region of Lake Lugano, but its models are both quaint and instructive, and, in their earnestness and number, unique. Where else could you hope to find the international headquarters of the Red Cross in Geneva, the Olympic bobsleigh run of

St Moritz and the Winkelried Monument of Stans? The only incongruity in the whole picturesque scene at Swissminiatur (unless one counts the scale model of the Mövenpick service station overhanging the A1 Motorway at Würenlos) is a plaster model of the *Titanic*. Swissminiatur amplifies a truth echoed by model villages worldwide: the gathering of reduced objects that would never be brought together under any other circumstance, save perhaps the Eurovision Song Contest, is just inherently comical.

But why go to all the trouble to visit these places if you can just go to Mini-Europe in Belgium and see almost everything in one go? One reason for not going to Mini-Europe is because Mini-Europe is terrible, and you must avoid it even if you have absolutely nothing else to do. Mini-Europe is what happens when a civic amusement is designed by a committee on which all the creative and sensible members have consistently called in sick, perhaps only too aware of what was being constructed on their watch. One is greeted at the entrance of Mini-Europe by a person dressed as a giant orange turtle administering unwanted hugs, and it's all grimness from there. One walks past a soulless array of more than 300 buildings from all the countries in the Union, including such cheering resin randomness as the Rock of Cashel in Tipperary, Anne Hathaway's Cottage in Stratford and a North Sea oil platform. Big Ben and the Eiffel Tower are also there of course, but they serve only to emphasise the odd choices elsewhere. (Not that the four-lane Adolphe Bridge in Luxembourg City or the aircraft-carrier stylings of the Oceanarium in Lisbon, founded 1998, aren't special things in their own right, it's more that they aren't necessarily on a par with their playmates the Coliseum and the Acropolis.) It turns out that some buildings are there because local councillors or tourist officers made financial arrangements for them to be included, a novel form of civic product placement.

Mini-Europe exemplifies a shrinking vision, a meaningless stamp collection. Even when it opened on the outskirts of Brussels with a certain optimism in 1989, no one could quite say what it was for. The launch brochure asked its visitors whether they were 'For or Against Europe?', which was only one remove from asking, 'The World. Yes or no?' On this evidence, I predict you will find yourself 100 per cent against. Mini-Europe is over-manicured and over-sponsored, and it is almost invulnerable to humanity, making you long for the idiosyncrasies of almost anywhere else. About 300,000 people visit it annually.

For the most laboriously rewarding and painstakingly authentic of all models we must return once more to Great Britain, specifically to the miniature village called Pendon in Oxfordshire. The work here is so laborious, and so authentic, that many decades since its birth in 1931 it is still very far from completion. Indeed, the idea of the model makers at Pendon 'putting the finishing touches' to their creation may fill them with horror. At Pendon, the thrill is the chase, and a dedicated team edge towards perfection at a pace that even snails would regard as cautious. A brochure from 1968 refers to that ominous day when all the Pendon modellers can finally go home: the model will not be finished, it says, but 'fulfilled', like a long-term promissory note.

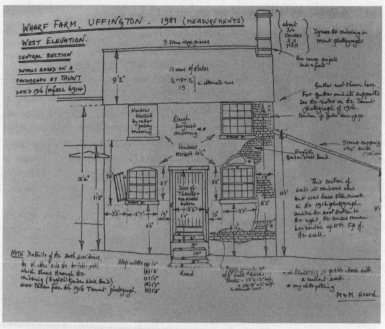

'Progress is slow': a scale plan for a farm building at Pendon.

Pendon is located in a two-storey concrete dwelling at Long Wittenham, near Abingdon, but some of it is also in Finickyland and Pedanticland, such is the exacting vision of its founder, the suitably named Roye England. England, an Australian, came to the area to live with relatives as a young man in 1925, and loved it so much that he never left. He was distressed to see some of the imminent changes in the landscape around the Vale of White Horse, not least the destruction of a thatched cottage nearby that was having its roof updated with pink asbestos. He resolved to preserve in miniature the beauty all around him, and he was not slapdash. That brochure from 1968 describes the modelling work as 'slow'; an updated brochure from 1990 still describes the work as 'slow', and mentions unspecified 'long delays and disappointments'. The later brochure shows Roye England at his 'modelling table', which very closely resembles an ordinary table, and behind him is a pile of detritus that would fill half a skip, lots of rolled-up paper plans and ledgers and files, and an unexpected print of a woman in a bonnet and lace. Roye England, by contrast, is in a shiny bomber jacket, and he's smiling as he holds up an unfinished cardboard house.

Slowly, a landscape of cottages and other buildings did emerge. Pendon (originally Pendon Parva or 'little village hall') began on a few tables in a youth hostel, but then expanded to an ex-RAF hut with leaking roof, before finally coming to rest in its present dry home. One early highlight was a sixteen-tier Brunel timber viaduct, though everything was really a highlight, such was the finesse and attention expended on each detail. In a playful interview with BBC Radio Oxford in 1971, Roye England described how he called on local farmers and shopkeepers to duplicate their buildings, climbing ladders and extending ropes to gain precise measurements (the model is scaled 4mm to the foot). He took a great many photos too, and remembered calling at the front door of one overgrown cottage to be greeted by a woman who, when asked whether she would let him take some pictures of her home, instructed England tersely to 'Ask him!' as she pointed across the garden to a man smoking a pipe in a shed. So England got to the shed and asked the man, and the man said, equally tersely, 'Ask her!'. When the modeller later told other villagers what had happened, one of them said, 'For goodness sake, don't go there, he'll murder you, he'll stab you!'

In an accent that sounded less Australian than it did John Gielgud, Roye England explained to the interviewer how he made one particular cottage wall from white cardboard. On this he had stuck many tiny paper bricks – each no bigger than a dash in this book. 'An architect who saw that piece of wall on the model said he thought [it] was thirteenth century,' England remembered, chuffed. He spoke of the 'frightfully fiddly' purple clematis above a cottage door with 201 leaves cut from greaseproof paper, the whole plant barely an inch high. Clearly we are entering the arena of instability here. 'There is a cat on the wall by the gate,' he continued in a clipped manner that suggested you wouldn't want to bring him bad news, 'that's made out of balsa wood. Its tail is cotton, its name is Skittles. It's a real cat that I measured up.' England explained that half the battle was thinking of original materials that could, when miniaturised out of complete context, be ingeniously adapted to the model. He said he was continually looking for the latest techniques to make things old.

He used human hair for thatched roofs, specifically Chinese hair, which was regarded as straighter and cheaper than English (pre-thatching, the hair was sent to Leeds University to be moth-proofed).

England died in 1995, by which time Pendon had become a committed team effort (England expected every man to do his duty). It had also become a registered museum, offering a tearoom alongside modelling updates from the helpful guides ('progress is slow'). Some scenes, including a railway station set in Dartmoor, are complete, but the principal 'Vale Scene' of working rural life that began it all is still being crafted. It is easy to mock the obsessiveness, of course, but it is a magnificent creation, a valuable historical record and a fine example of the miniature as an educational tool. It says: this is how things were then. In fact, better: this, to the very best of our ability, is *precisely* as things were then. One clipped box hedge is made from a surgical rubber sponge intended for the treatment of varicose ulcers.

The golden age of modelling has not passed, but the golden age of pleasantness probably has. If the Pendon modellers were to begin anew today, for example, they might be working alongside Jimmy Cauty, who has built an exquisite if violent alternative to the rural idyll and called it The Aftermath Dislocation Principle. This is a minutely detailed scene of about 5,000 police officers, jams of emergency vehicles with flashing lights, and a mass of media attention from camera crews. The model is scaled at 1:87, and represents one bleak square mile of ruined scrubland and concrete tower block. It is not quite clear what we are looking at, except for the fact that the scene occurs after a traumatic event. But what was the event? Have we just missed a terrible accident or a public insurgence? Or could this be just another ordinary day under a police state? Its purpose, other than as art, is also vague (its location is precise, however: Bedfordshire, at the historic heart of England). It was once the centrepiece model village at Banksy's Dismaland anti-theme park in Weston-super-Mare, and was then split into three shipping containers, the largest 40 feet long, to tour locations in the UK that had witnessed riots (visitors peered in through the containers' portholes). The model suggests the failure of a nation. Its perimeters are not hedged, fenced or trellised; they just roughly disintegrate, as if its inhabitants are about to fall off a cliff, or perhaps already have.

Cauty was a member of the provocative band KLF and the situationist art group K Foundation (which, most famously, burnt £1m in cash on a Scottish island and aimed machine guns at the audience at the Brit Awards), and it was always unlikely that a model village in his hands was going to be a walk in the park. He says he's happy for viewers to bring their own story to the scene, aware that any authored explanation may limit the demands of close observation. One close observation of his own: he notes the degree to which our urban landscapes have come to be dominated by hi-vis jackets:

construction workers are knocking things down, and security men huddle in imposing gangs, and police officers stir a sense of emergency. It's not a place where women will feel at ease, nor anyone for that matter, but seldom can a police state have seemed so visually compelling. Look, you say – a lorry has crashed into McDonald's, a cow has wandered into a building, a policeman is attacking another policeman with a pitchfork. Each new horror encourages dark delight. We do not, as Claude Lévi-Strauss contended, comprehend the entire object at once, but instead indulge in its cumulative revelations.

One headless policeman has made its way from Cauty's workshop to the desk of Tim Dunn, an expert on model villages in the UK (not a huge field, but a dedicated one). Dunn spent many years working at Bekonscot (a variety of jobs from the age of twelve: train operator, model builder, and birthday project manager during its seventy-fifth year), and his experience has made him an obvious port of call when redundant villages need a new home for obsolete models. In 2004 he received a call from a friend who works at Legoland: she said the Model World section at Thorpe Park in Surrey was being auctioned. This was a chance to acquire one's very own Eiffel Tower or Nelson's Column or the dramatic *Motherland Calls* sculpture that commemorated the Battle of Stalingrad, all going to make way for a rollercoaster named Stealth. Clearly none of these models was ideal for Bekonscot, but Tim Dunn was encouraged by the low auction estimates and the possibility of hosting a miniature Eiffel Tower in his front room, albeit at the height of 9 feet. It was made of steel. He won it for

£50, and set off in a van with friends to bring it home. When they arrived they found it wasn't 9 feet high as advertised, but 9 metres (Dunn remembers someone at Thorpe Park actually saying to him 'Oh silly me!'). He and his friends could only manage to transport the top two-thirds, and for the last twelve years the tower has resided in his uncle's back garden in Buckinghamshire. Dunn and his uncle (and presumably his uncle's neighbours) consider themselves fortunate that they didn't also acquire the Colosseum and the Pyramid of Cheops.

When I asked Dunn about the motivation behind these miniature worlds, he answered without hesitation. 'Frustration,' he said. 'Modellers may be frustrated about the past or the future. They might be seeking solace. It could be that they're trying to control the future by building a three-dimensional utopia, a genuine model model village.'

When we met, Dunn, who works for the rail booking company Trainline, was 'putting the finishing touches' to a book that got to the very heart of the matter. It was called *Model Villages*. It covered the tiny waterfront, from one of the earliest model villages (c.1908) in the garden of a London house, to the more recent efforts at the Museum of Power in Essex. What Dunn liked in particular were the furthest and quirkiest shores, such as the place in Dorset called Tinkleford, which wasn't on public display because it was made from flaking pink asbestos. He revelled in Little Italy, a private passion in the Welsh mountains in which a man who once went on holiday has created his homage to the Bridge of Sighs and the Tower of Pisa from mannequins and bits of bread oven. Dunn also enjoyed the model villages that went the extra mile, or 1/87th of a mile, by placing a model village within itself. Ideally that model village also contained a model village, and one could carry on reducing and incorporating like a Russian doll, until one ended up with a village green the size of a flattened pea, or smaller.

'I think it's a bit like gardening – the desire to tame and beautify,' Dunn concludes. 'And you mustn't deride how people find their happiness. Many people with Asperger's and autism find pleasure and a level of safety in making or looking at models, and if you're an introvert, how better to spend your time? But it can also be the most sociable activity, because you're showing what you can do, asking for conversation, exhibiting and making yourself open to criticism or praise. You could argue that the most reclusive hobby, and the least social, is reading books, but no one regards readers of books as misfits or socially inadequate.'

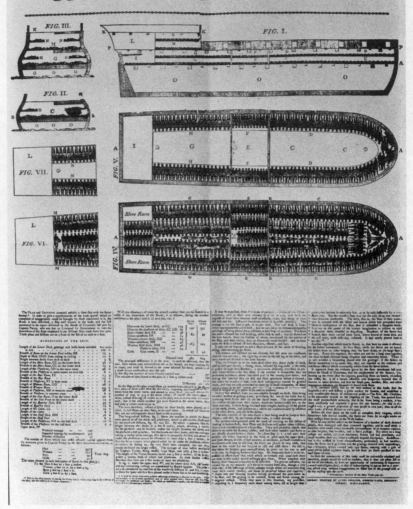

The unsafe passage: the true terrors of the slave ship 'Brooks' revealed in 1789.

Mini-break, 1789:
England's Slave Ships

At the end of the eighteenth century, anyone who knew anything about the degree of human suffering caused by the slave trade resolved to put an end to it. Reformers were appalled at the way Africans were crammed and shackled in hulls as they crossed the ocean to the New World, a system both cruel and often fatal, and they were convinced that as soon as these deprivations were exposed they would summarily end not only the inhumane method of transport but the slave trade as a whole. The cause of basic human decency would triumph over the shameful manifestations of avarice. What a naive proposition.

It took many decades for the reformers to win their argument. Even when abolitionist petitions were first presented to the British parliament in the 1780s, the hardest and longest of struggles lay ahead. The time was judged not right, both politically and economically. High moral ambitions were defeated by base personal interests. The case was finally won by the tireless efforts of several men over two decades, and by a marketing campaign that was so simple, and had so much impact, that its two overriding messages still ring true: show, don't tell; and, if possible, show it in miniature.

On 12 May 1789, William Wilberforce, the twenty-nine-year-old MP for Yorkshire, delivered a speech in the House of Commons that has come to be regarded as one of the most important texts in British history, alongside Magna Carta, the King James Bible, Darwin's *On the Origin of Species* and Crick and Watson's first proof of DNA. The problem is, no full record of the speech survives, and we have only the most fragmentary accounts of what he said. The speech lasted approximately three and a half hours and was delivered largely off the cuff. The most reliable report appears in William Cobbett's *Parliamentary History*, from which we may appreciate the modest and humble approach of a member tackling his first significant campaign.

'I mean not to accuse anyone,' he began, 'but to take the shame upon myself, in common indeed with the whole parliament of Great Britain, for having suffered this horrid trade to be carried on under their authority. We are all guilty.' The guilt he felt pertained to the slave trade as a whole, but in particular to the conditions under which slaves were transported: 'So much misery condensed in so little room is more than the human imagination had ever before conceived.' He was referring to what became known as the 'Middle Passage', that part of the triangular trade route that shipped slaves from the west coast of Africa to the sugar, cotton and tobacco plantations of the Caribbean and the Americas. Again, he was keen not to apportion blame. He believed, or claimed to believe, that slave traders in Liverpool must be excused for their abominable actions, 'For I verily believe . . . if the wretchedness of any one of the many hundred negroes stowed in each ship could be brought before their view . . . that there is no one among them whose heart would bear it.'

Wilberforce was a recent convert to the cause. The initial impetus for reform came in the middle of the eighteenth century from the Quakers. Early abolitionists such as Granville Sharp, James Ramsay and Sir Charles Middleton may all lay claim to having influenced Wilberforce in his early days as an MP; American abolitionist Quakers, fired with Revolutionary zeal, may also stake a claim. But it was Thomas Clarkson, a young Anglican churchman from Cambridgeshire, who exerted the greatest single impact on both Wilberforce and the campaign. Clarkson's interest in slavery began as an academic study (as an entry in a student essay competition), but it soon became his life's polemical work. His descriptions of the conditions onboard the slave ships – the extent of dysentery and other diseases, the attitude to death as an occupational hazard – drew something from Dante's nine circles of hell.

Meeting Wilberforce at a dinner party, Clarkson presented him with a large and elaborate gift – a chest full of African objects, including cotton, dyes, pepper, knives and musical instruments, all of which he believed could make a fine replacement for slaves in the triangular trade. The box also contained manacles, whips and other objects of torture used to control both black captives and white sailors by sadistic naval captains. It was a brilliant and provocative visual aid. But the most significant was yet to come.

Despite his eloquence, and the measured tone of his arguments, and the seemingly incontestable moral human *rightness* of his case, Wilberforce's landmark speech did not lead to a motion for abolition. Instead, debate was adjourned, and, in that most deadly of delaying tactics, the issue was referred to a committee. Wilberforce's subsequent diary entry was comical in its nonchalance: 'Slave business put off till next year.'

Wilberforce suffered debilitating health problems but resolved to fight on. He realised that slavery was an issue so deeply entrenched in the economic welfare of the country that it would take more than well-considered words to effect change (Great Britain had assumed control of the principal African slave trade from Portugal more than a century before, but other empires, including the French, Spanish and Dutch, also ran their colonies with slave labour). Taking his cues from Thomas Clarkson, Wilberforce acknowledged that parliamentary reform would only be possible with a mass mobilisation of public opinion, and realised that public opinion would only be swayed by something other than words. This additional element arrived in the mass-produced form of a vivid illustration, and in the shape of a handmade miniature wooden model.

In 1788, a banker and amateur artist named William Elford toured the Liverpool dockyards to discover for himself the extent of deprivation, and asked a British naval officer for the dimensions of a slave ship named *Brooks* (later commonly also known as *Brookes*). He found that a recent parliamentary act restricting the quantity of human cargo was indeed having an effect: before the act, the ship had carried 609 slaves, and it was now only allowed to carry 454. Using these figures, Elford set about drawing what he imagined the below-decks layout of *Brooks* to be. And in this way, and with a terrible irony, the relative ameliorations in stowage capacity served to bring to light the true horrors of the Middle Passage.

The illustration split the boat horizontally across the lower decks, with one part showing almost 300 figures shackled together with no space between them, and insufficient space above them to sit up. A second drawing showed how the cargo was divided into men, women and boys, and how a platform above the main hold (in the manner of galleries in a church) held a ring of 130 additional slaves, with 2 feet and 7 inches between their wooden boards and the beam above. They were coffin ships. Elford's work drew on his training as a draughtsman (he was a Royal Academician), but his neat plan was a neat fiction. Technically it was inaccurate (a ship modeller would have noticed the overly thick planking), and it rendered the slaves inert if not completely lifeless; it was, as the historian of slavery Marcus Wood puts it, practically a slave trader's utopia, depicting as it did the most passive bodies willingly manoeuvred into the smallest space. But it was also a design with resonance, an image, in Wood's phrase, 'which invites a viewer to fill in its emotional blankness'. It was this element that partly accounts for its phenomenal impact and lasting success – that and the fact that, as with other miniatures we've already encountered, it encouraged the viewer to look very closely at a subject previously ignored or unexamined in detail. It was bold visual literacy for the masses, and the masses (as much as a quarter of the adult male population in some regions) put their names to reforming petitions. The battle for the abolition of the slave trade stands as the first large-scale British human rights campaign; for the first time, and despite the passivity of their depiction, Africans were promoted as fellow humans rather than tradable commodities. By bringing the ship down to scale, the misery of the souls onboard was amplified.

Clarkson seized on the *Brooks* illustration and commissioned (or perhaps even drew himself) a more accomplished version with a further cross section of the crammed poop deck. He may also have been responsible for adding the text to the diagram, explaining (as if it needed it) the precise dimensions of the ship and the inadequate space for its cargo. With the aid of the principal abolitionist society in London he also ensured its widespread dissemination. Important advances in printing enabled cheaper and more detailed plate impressions: 1,700 were published as a single-sheet copper engraving, 7,000 were printed from a woodblock. The image was adapted for a further large-scale printing in Philadelphia. Most significantly, the illustration was also reproduced in the rapidly expanding network of local newspapers.

A few weeks after Wilberforce's speech in 1789, Thomas Clarkson travelled to France to meet abolitionists in Paris, only to find that the cause was even less advanced than in Britain; predictably, almost all reforming energies were subsumed by the turbulence of the Revolution. He brought with him many prints of the *Brooks* ship, and while Louis XVI was understood to be sympathetic to the cause, he was judged too frail to view the horrors of the illustration. Clarkson thus gathered his principal support for abolition from Marquis de Lafayette, one of the architects of the American Revolution, and his revolutionary colleague Comte de Mirabeau. Mirabeau was so impressed by the *Brooks* print that he commissioned a yard-long wooden model of the ship, complete with a collection of tiny figures representing the packed slaves. He also prepared a speech for the French National Assembly: 'Behold the model of a vessel laden with these unfortunate beings, and seek not to turn away your gaze! How they are piled one upon the other! How they are crammed into the between-decks! Unable to stand erect: nay, even seated, their heads are bowed . . .'

The meeting at which his speech was to be delivered was cancelled after pressure from a trading lobby; it is clear from the printed version that his fire was undimmed. 'Mark how the vessel when it rolls hurts them, mutilates them, bruises them against each other, tears them with their own chains, and presents thus a thousand tortures . . . The poor wretches! I see them, I hear them gasping for breath . . .'

The model helped us see them too. Wilberforce also had a wooden slave ship made (its maker is unknown). He used it at Select Committee hearings in 1790 and 1791, and passed it around the front benches during subsequent debates in the House of Commons. It was about half the length of Mirabeau's model, and in the place of the removable slave figures were layers of pasted down cut-outs from the printed illustration. The effect was no less shocking to those who saw it; indeed, a horrific awareness took hold, something all the previous talk couldn't match.

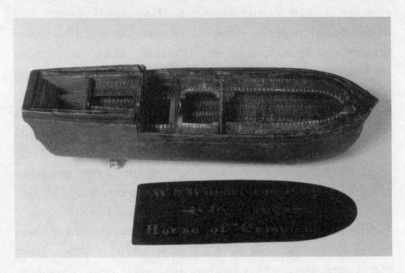

Clarkson had spent dangerous months at many British ports gathering evidence for the parliamentary battles, and inevitably found very few traders willing to help. Occasionally a ship owner or ship cleaner offered useful information, and writers, painters and poets (including George Morland and William Cowper) weighed in too. Josiah Wedgwood mass-produced a powerful cameo in relief (in the shape of brooches, medallions and plaques) of a kneeling shackled slave. But nothing had the direct parliamentary impact of the model: it was simply the most tactile representation of human misery, and to those who held it the reality was undeniable: they held the fate of humanity in their hands.

The longer the debates raged, the more the packed *Brooks* (and many others like it) sailed on. The slave trade was finally abolished in 1807, or at least Britain's endorsement of it. Wilberforce became a popular hero and a history lesson favourite, and in time Thomas Clarkson and the other 'saints' also received their due. The latter years of the Napoleonic Wars saw a grand effort to convince France and other European powers to follow the British lead in abolition. The image of *Brooks* maintained its position as a powerful tool; only after Pope Pius VII saw it in 1815 did he resolve to speak out against the trade in Portugal and Spain. Portuguese trafficking ended within months; the French ceased all trading in 1818, the Spanish two years later.

The passing of an act, however heroic it may seem, does not succeed in wiping the memory clean. A scale illustration and a wooden model, vital as they were, cannot hope to eradicate the centuries of brutalism. But as a reminder of effect and progress the artefacts are miniature explosions. The model Wilberforce passed around parliament now resides beneath a case in Wilberforce House in Hull, the reformer's birthplace. Older readers may recall the ship's brief cameo in the final episode of the groundbreaking 1969 television series *Civilisation*; others may find disturbing contemporary echoes in the migrant ships today seeking safe harbour in the Mediterranean.

All love is vanity: Richard Cosway's flattering portrait
of the Prince of Wales.

Chapter Three

Portrait of a Marriage

In January 1796, the Prince of Wales decided he would take only one thing with him when he died. Writing in his will, he requested to be buried with precisely what he was wearing at the moment of his death, which happened to be a night-gown and a gold locket around his neck containing a portrait of Maria Fitzherbert, his one true love ('My wife! My wife of my heart and soul!'). The locket was ornate and elaborate: oval-shaped, 37mm high, surrounded by eighteen rose-cut diamonds with six more on the suspension loop. Within it was a portrait on ivory by Richard Cosway, who was regarded by the aristocracy as the finest miniaturist in the world.

Thirty-four years after composing his will, the Prince – who by the time of his death had ruled as King George IV for ten years – got his wish. He was buried at Windsor in 1830 with the portrait of Fitzherbert 'placed right upon my heart'. One of his executors, the Duke of Wellington, saw him laid out with it on his deathbed; the Duke was one of the few to know the whole story.

George had apparently fallen in love with Maria Fitzherbert the first time he saw her from a carriage in 1780, but only began his pursuit after a chance meeting at the opera four years later. The Prince had a reputation as a dandy and spendthrift, and Maria, six years his senior, was slow to return his affections. The Prince, who also had a reputation for capriciousness, devised a chivalrous if deranged plan to woo her: he stabbed himself in the chest, and his emissaries informed Maria that he would remove his bandages (and risk death) if she didn't come to him at Carlton House at once. Maria went. According to her cousin and biographer William Stourton, she was overwhelmed with shock at the pale and desperate Prince, and the shock was compounded when he asked Georgiana, Duchess of Devonshire (whom Maria had brought along as a chaperone) for a ring for Maria's finger. Maria, under duress, tried it on for size, and then agreed to marry him. And the next day she regretted it, and fled to the Low Countries with the hope that the whole thing would blow over.

It didn't. Their subsequent relationship was tempestuous, and necessarily conducted in secret. Their wedding was forbidden by at least two statutes – she was Catholic, and she had not been approved by the Prince's father, King George III – and it proceeded only when the disgraced curate John Burt was sprung from Fleet Prison to perform the ceremony. The taverns were abuzz with the gossip – it was the worst-kept secret in town. And the drinkers could be cruel: they repeated Georgiana's depiction of him as 'inclined to be too fat and looks much like a woman in men's cloaths', and of her 'determined' chin and ill-fitting false teeth.

The Prince's passion for Fitzherbert rose and fell; modern historians paint his desires as both sexual and maternal. In 1785, while still in the first flushes of wooing, he wrote her a forty-two-page love letter with guarantees to 'fly upon ye wings of love' and be 'ye best of husbands . . . unalterably thine'; he also threatened to kill himself if his desire wasn't reciprocated. He had affairs during their marriage, but he usually returned with regrets and promises. It all appeared to be over by 1795, when Prince George agreed to marry Princess Caroline of Brunswick, but this official – if bigamous – coupling lasted barely a year. (He had agreed to the marriage only when his father offered in return to clear his huge debts. There certainly wasn't much passion involved: catching sight of Princess Caroline on their wedding day, the Prince was heard to say, 'I'm not well! Pray, get me a glass of brandy.')

As well as the portrait that accompanied him to his grave, between 1784 and 1792 Prince George commissioned at least four other miniatures of Fitzherbert from Richard Cosway, for which he paid about 30 guineas each (about £1,500 today). One of them featured nothing more than a milky portrait of her right eye. Prince George also believed that Fitzherbert might appreciate a portrait of Prince George, so Cosway painted that too, and it was presented to her in the same type of glittering locket that we've already seen: oval-shaped, twenty-four rose-cut diamonds, the ivory portrait protected not by glass or crystal but by a large 'portrait diamond', the whole thing almost certainly made – like the matching locket around King George's neck when he died – by the royal jewellers Rundell, Bridge & Rundell. In early July 2017 I held it in the palm of my hand, and it felt like treasure.

It was part of an upcoming auction at Christie's in London called 'The Exceptional Sale', an irregular grouping of valuable objects that might easily have appeared in other specialist auctions but were judged so narratively unique that they might attract buyers not usually interested in, say, portrait lockets. Other items in the sale included a pair of stirrups that were believed to have been used by William III at the Battle of the Boyne in 1690, and two marble lions commissioned by Charles V of France for his tomb at the Basilica of St Denis in Paris. The stirrups would fail to meet their reserve estimate of £40,000–£60,000, while the lions would fetch more than £9.3m. But how much would the locket go for?

'One *is* immediately drawn to it – the ultimate love token,' Jo Langston said as she removed it from the display case during a sale preview. Langston was Christie's head of portrait miniatures, and she had become entranced by the locket during the six months she had spent researching its history at the London Library nearby. She learnt of the stabbing that drew them together, and how George had grown quite insistent in the days before his death that his burial request would be granted. She also traced the lineage of the portrait from Maria Fitzherbert's adopted daughter Minney Seymour to the current vendor, a more distant family member.

The portrait shows the Prince with tousled hair and dappled cheeks. His face is turned a quarter outward, towards the locket clasp, and he looks optimistic in military garb, with protective armour covering his upper chest and neck. Perhaps a war is raging beyond; perhaps the battle is in his head. We don't know if it was painted from life, but quite possibly. 'These days we don't make portrait miniatures,' Langston reflected, 'but we often have a photo of our loved one on the lock-screen of our phones.' The portrait is still luminescent, and has not faded with exposure to light. 'There's never been a comparable item on the market. We need to do justice to the piece, but we can't price it at such a level that it puts people off. Value-wise, it helps that it has this scandalous story attached to it. I told it to one woman recently and she started welling up.' Holding the locket in my hand, two words came to mind: 'flash' and 'priceless'. The usual estimate for a nice Cosway at auction would be £4,000–£6,000. The estimate here was £80,000–£120,000.

For the royal family, Richard Cosway painted big and small. He had been artistic adviser to the Prince of Wales for many years before completing the his 'n' hers miniatures, painting not only people but also an elaborate ceiling at Carlton House. Cosway made almost fifty miniatures for the Prince, and George's patronage led to commissions from all upper branches of society. In 1789 he painted the Duke of Clarence, the future William IV; in 1804 Louis-Philippe, the future king of France. In 1808 he turned his hand to Arthur Wellesley (later the Duke of Wellington), a study in a scarlet tunic just before the start of the Peninsular War.

At more than 7cm, Richard Cosway's miniatures were often slightly larger than his predecessors', but it was his characteristic compositional traits that made him popular amongst his wealthy clientele. His biographer Stephen Lloyd has noted how Cosway deliberately enlarged his sitters' eyes and increased the size of their head in comparison with their body. His choice of misty sky-blue backgrounds flattered similarly. 'These representations, which are both glamorous and intimate, can be seen as the mirror in which elite Regency society saw itself reflected.' Lloyd quotes William Hazlitt: Cosway's miniatures 'were not fashionable – they were fashion itself'.

His perfectionism, and the pleasure he took in his work, was best described by the diarist William Hickey. Cosway painted as many as twelve sitters a day, but when Hickey's mistress Charlotte Barry turned up in December 1781 he took a full three hours.

He led her into his painting room, rubbed out the elegantly arranged hair, and drew her exactly as she sat before me, making as he had truly predicted one of the most beautiful pictures I ever beheld, the likeness being inimitable. With some difficulty I prevailed upon him not to touch it any more . . . but that he would not hear of, saying he must touch the drapery a little, besides which he was too proud of his performance not to be desirous of showing it to a few persons . . .

Cosway was part of a storied lineage. Miniaturists had served the royal family since a court painter named Jean Clouet established the practice in France in the 1520s (intriguingly, he was known to his clients principally as Janet, as was his son). At the English court a family from Ghent known as Hornebolte (sometimes Horenbout) established themselves as miniaturists at about the same time, and became favourites of Henry VIII. Lucas Hornebolte painted the King in miniature at least four times, and his work set the style for more than a century: delicate watercolour brushwork on vellum, usually head and shoulders (rather than full face), more circular than oval. He was also the main tutor of Hans Holbein the Younger, enabling the German artist to adapt his full-size portraits to a smaller scale. It was Holbein's flattering palm-size depiction of Anne of Cleves that suggested to Henry VIII that she might be a suitable replacement for Jane Seymour in 1540; alas, her appearance in the flesh did not live up to her miniature.

The art of the portrait miniature was known originally as 'limning', and emerged as a hybrid of manuscript illustration. Early examples were worn as medals, and often presented as aristocratic calling cards. Both Henry VIII and Elizabeth I presented likenesses of themselves to foreign royals, and George IV revived the tradition. But most early practitioners, including Holbein and the Flemish manuscript artist Levina Teerlinc, regarded themselves not as miniaturists, but as exceptional painters who occasionally painted small (Henry VIII referred to Teerlinc, one of the few prominent female painters, as his 'paintrix'). The true miniature only established itself as a distinct art form in the 1570s, when a man named Nicholas Hilliard came to town.

Hilliard was born in Devon in 1547. He was the son of a goldsmith, which no doubt hastened his appreciation of filigree detail. The first of his miniatures we know of were painted around the age of twelve, and they display a distinct talent for what was still regarded as an uncommon practice; one critic would dismiss the miniature as 'personal furniture'. Those who saw Hilliard's more mature work were entranced: he painted not just regular portraits for the most ruffed female Elizabethans, but also full-length depictions of devotional young men – works unnamed by the artist but now popularly referred to as 'Young Man Against Flames' and 'Man Clasping a Hand from a Cloud'. These were symbolic images, but they were realised precisely, with intricate lacework and jewellery. He left us a full description of his methods (he used a gum solution to secure his water-based pigments to vellum, and occasionally liquid gold), and in 1600 he explained the appeal of miniature work as a whole. 'Limning, a thing apart,' he claimed, 'which excelleth all other painting whatsoever.'

The historian Katherine Coombs describes how Hilliard also defined his work as 'a kind of gentle painting', by which he meant refined and becoming. It was work, he suggested, that wasn't all-consuming, a pursuit a gentleman 'may leave when he will'. Moreover, he wrote, 'it is secret: a man may use it, and scarcely be perceived of his own folk.' The word 'miniature' only became popular after 1627, when the painter and critic Edward Norgate wrote a thesis entitled *Miniatura, or the Art of Limning*; the word soon moved beyond painting to become associated with anything small.

Norgate also explained how the miniaturist must not only possess great skill as a painter, but also a certain temperament: 'The practicer of limning,' he counselled, should be 'preizly pure and klenly in all his doings . . . At the least let your apparel be silke, such as sheadeth lest dust or haires, weare nothing straight, and take heed of the dandrawe of the head sheading from the hairs.' And don't talk while painting, Norgate advised, lest any flecks of spit alight on your werke, after which the entire of said werke would have to be abandon'd and thrown on heape.

What was the appeal of the miniature portrait? As a fancy, it was the precursor of the Swiss watch: only the wealthy could afford to commission and sit for one, and the very wealthy could afford to commission a large amount. The aristocracy used them as calling cards, swapping them in the same way that captains of football teams exchange pennants before an international. George IV couldn't give away enough of his Cosways: Prince Blücher and Count Platov both pinned his portraits to their chest and wore them as gallantry medals. Women generally wore their portraits as one might a wedding ring – relationship status spoken for. Men were more reticent about their love tokens, usually concealing them on a ribbon beneath their shirt. George IV wore Maria Fitzherbert in this way, as did Nelson with Emma Hamilton (when they struggled to seal his fatal wound in 1805, eyewitnesses reported seeing her still by his heart). Above all, miniatures were convenient, their portability easing an absence. No one found them more convenient than Shakespeare, who used them to advance a plot and reveal or conceal a true identity. 'Here, wear this jewel for me, 'tis my picture,' Olivia entreats the disguised Viola in *Twelfth Night*. In *Hamlet*, the Prince demands that his mother contrast two miniatures of his father and stepfather: 'Look here upon this picture, and on this / The counterfeit presentment of two brothers.'

As with other, later, miniature obsessions, the art attracted its fair share of outsiders. Richard Gibson, one of the leading miniaturists of the seventeenth century, initially signed his work D.G.; D may have stood for the diminutive Dick, but it may equally have been Dwarf. As well as being celebrated for his miniatures, Gibson was celebrated also for his own size: 3 feet 10 inches. Gibson painted both Charles I and Oliver Cromwell, but he achieved fame by two other routes: when he married a woman named Anna of the exact same height their wedding became the stuff of poetry and intrigue, as did their five children of regular height. The second incident was operatic. Abraham van der Doort, the keeper of the king's pictures, was entrusted, in the summer of 1640, with the Gibson miniature *The Parable of the Lost Sheep*. Somehow he managed to mislay it, and was so distraught at the loss that he saw but one way out: Van der Doort hanged himself rather than face Charles I's wrath. The painting turned up shortly afterwards.

The aristocratic mania for miniatures subsided in the mid-nineteenth century; those in search of a good likeness turned instead to photography (and for a less faithful one to Impressionism). Reversing what Hilliard believed, painting in miniature was increasingly considered unmanly, and, coupled with the booming pleasures of the doll's house, widely accepted as a quiet and acceptable hobby for women. These days, miniatures may frequently appear as clichéd set dressing; no adaptation of Austen or Brontë seems complete without miniatures scattered on a desk or wall. Characters in the novels gaze upon them as one might a family snapshot, or Snapchat.

But the exceptional miniature may still arrest our heart. The Cosway portrait of George IV faced its public at Christie's on 6 July 2017, and the opening bid immediately overtook the artist's previous record at auction. But it was going much higher, and the successful bidder (a private collector) ended up with an invoice, including all fees, for £341,000. The portrait may never be seen in public again, its romantic entanglements palmed away like an illusionist's trick.

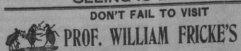

Mini-break, 1851:
Hamburg's Talented Fleas

In the first half of 1851, the construction of a colossal dome began to block out the sun in London's Leicester Square, and it was promoted with much hoopla and greeted with much scepticism. Inside the dome was a 60-foot diameter globe, and inside the globe was a zigzag of stairs from which, as one ascended each step and gazed at the impressions and information on the perimeter walls, one could discover much about the shape and variety of the world. There was no Antarctica yet, but the Arctic featured near the ventilation system at the top, and on the way to the top there was much on the darkness of Africa and the civilising forces of Europe. The globe was also an exposition of size and scale: how vast and wondrous was our world, how small we were as we walked within it. And then, by spending a whole day within it, during which we could travel within four continents, one could blow all those concepts of size and scale to nothing.

The globe was the idea of a man named James Wyld, a commercial mapmaker and sometime Member of Parliament for Bodmin, Cornwall. The construction cost between £13,000 and £20,000, a colossally risky outlay, but Wyld's investors recouped their investment many times over: more than a million people paid to traipse through it within its first year (it lasted ten). One of these visitors was a correspondent from *Punch*, who, having experienced Wyld's world in miniature, pondered how it might appear to a visitor from Mars. He found that the world was closed every Sunday, and that it had only nine full-time inhabitants, including a pageboy with bright buttons. The world had no revolutions, as in France, and 'no insults, as in America'.

Six months after Wyld's world opened it had competition from another attraction in Leicester Square that also played with scale. This one claimed it was 'The Greatest Novelty in London', to which the only logical response should be, 'Of course it was – it was a flea circus.' And not just any flea circus, but a flea circus featuring Herr Lidusdroph's '200 Fleas of All Nations'. What could they do? What *couldn't* they do! They could form themselves into Russian artillery 'firing off cannon'. Eight fleas could pull a stagecoach with a coachman and guard (the coachman and guard were also fleas). A 'Russian Hercules' carried twelve fleas on his back. And then, presumably as a finale, there was 'The Patriot Kossuth mounted on an Austrian Flea' (or, as the graphic poster had it, 'an Austrian Flee'). Admission was the same as to James Wyld's globe: one shilling. How would you not rush to see this show?

Herr Lidusdroph didn't have the flea scene all to himself. His main competitor, and perhaps his inspiration, may have been Signor Louis Bertolotto, whose show appeared in

London, Canada and New York, and featured 'industrious' and 'educated' fleas who dressed as Wellington and Napoleon, and, in a subsequent performance, as Don Quixote and Sancho Panza. (You may justifiably raise an eyebrow over the 'Herr' and the 'Signor', but they were showmen: Bertolotto came from either London or Wales, and there was more than one of them running circuses in different countries at the same time, perhaps as Bartolotto or Bartoletti.) One of the Bertolottos noted in his memoirs that the male flea was lazy, and he only used female ones; when he presented 'a little brunette on a sofa . . . flirting with a fashionable beau while her mama's mind is engaged in the politics of a newspaper', the fact that all of the performers were female suddenly seemed insignificant.

And then there was Professor William Fricke from the early 1900s, who claimed to run 'the only show of its kind in the world', although we already know otherwise. But Fricke's show was unique in the extent of his troupe – 300 fleas compared to Herr Lidusdroph's measly 200 – and in the nature of his specialties: his fleas not only walked a tightrope, operated a mill, ran a merry-go-round and presented a 'Large Pantomime Ballet in Ladies Costume'. According to Fricke's poster, the show demonstrated 'what 41 years of most tedious work has accomplished'. But the audience was jumpy, and had to be reassured: the poster also claimed 'there is no danger of any desertion in our flea family!'. There was also a guarantee that all the fleas were 'alive and living . . . not mechanical'. Most impressive of all, 'every flea has its own name'. (One can only assume this meant 300 different names, rather than one name, such as Sunny Jim, given to all 300. But one had to attend the show to find out for sure.)

The poster announced that the flea circus came *direct* from Hamburg, Germany. In other words, it did not get waylaid in Amsterdam or Paris, and the fleas were not permitted downtime at the Folies Bergères, for example, or the Tuileries. But even fleas – especially fleas, perhaps – risk burnout, so hard have they worked at their pantomime ballet and high-wire acts, and so far have they extended their abilities beyond the expectations of their genus. If all this appears preposterous or surreal, then I would suggest that you have not fully attuned yourself to the realities of the performing flea or the principles of the flea market, and I fear we may have to begin the story from scratch.

The flea circus was a real and vivid thing, by turns glamorous and pathetic, and Victorians ruined their eyes trying to make one and see one. There were circuses with mechanical magnetic fleas, and some where fleas were replaced by wind and thin wires, or by dust, but most presented at least some of what their marketing material offered. Fleas could indeed fight a duel, although not of their own volition: a trainer tied a piece of wire to the legs of two fleas, placed them within a tall jar, and exhibited it as combat sport; in reality, the fleas were just trying to rid themselves of their appendages. A flea could be made to seem like he/she was driving a tiny cart or carriage by attaching a vehicle to its torso; the fleas then pulled, after a bit of a struggle, an object many times their weight. And fleas did appear to jump through hoops, and walk a tightrope, not because they had been trained to do so, but because they had been so restrained: once released from their containers and harnessed to props, what else could they do but struggle and heave and jump?

'They live off me and I live off them': Prof. William Heckler's fleas at Hubert's Museum on West 42nd Street.

Even the most elaborate flea circus could quite happily fit within a suitcase. It was usually laid out in the manner of a full-size ring, with the high wire overhead and traditional stripy garishness all around, but the act itself has its origins in a more sedate pursuit. The first example is believed to have been created in 1578 by a London jeweller named Mark

Scaliot, who hatched a new way of displaying the dexterity and detail of his craft: he would hitch a lock or locket or ring to a flea to show it off and demonstrate how light it was. Other jewellers followed; for them, harnessing a flea to a piece of jewellery was as easy as putting a finger through a ring. They fed the fleas in the traditional way – from the blood in their arm. As one flea impresario later put it, 'they live off me, and I live off them'.

The appeal of the tiny circus was rich and varied, but at the core there was wonder. How could one not marvel that such a thing was even possible? How could one not admire the dedication required to mount such an absurd piece of drama? The flea circus thrived at a time before irony, and if our admiration mingled with scepticism perhaps it was only because we wished the scepticism to be overcome. The familiar traits of miniaturisation were all intact: a desire for mastery and control; a fixation on the seemingly impossible; the studied patience that brought forth astonishment. As French philosopher Gaston Bachelard put it, 'the smarter I am at miniaturising the world, the better I possess it'. But there was one difference. Unlike most other miniatures, the reduction in scale was not an end in itself: for a small circus was still a circus, and there was still money and a living to be made. Hoopla was all, and competition was avid: if the tent next door had the Wild Man of Borneo and the Woman with Three Hearts, the more your fleas resembled Sancho Panza and Napoleon the better.

The magician and historian of magic Ricky Jay has noted

in his quarterly newsletter that rivalry between flea circuses was once so fierce – in addition to the fleamasters mentioned above, he uncovered performances orchestrated by men named Kitichingman, Likonti, Ubini, Günther, and Englaca – that publicity agents were engaged to draw up fanciful stories that might elevate one attraction above another. One such, placed by a huckster for a show at Reynolds's Exhibition in Liverpool, offered a £10 reward for the return of a flea much missed by 'his sorrowing friends'. What caused the desertion? 'It appears that his mind has been affected by nervous shock caused by a recent accident while essaying the daring act of Looping the Double Loop on a Motor, and he has lately been suffering from a certain malady which has affected his naturally lively and energetic temperament, producing severe mental depression.' How to distinguish this depressed flea from any other? 'When last seen [he] was wearing a gold collar and chain, and he answers to the name of "Sunny Jim".' Early in the twentieth century, in another PR stunt so pure in conception that one dearly wanted it to be true, a flea belonging to William Heckler's show in Times Square was reported to have checked into the Waldorf Astoria under the name The Great Herman.

Fleamasters discovered that only the human flea (*Pulex irritans*), as opposed to the cat or dog flea, was sufficiently large and intelligent to carry on circus duties. Bertolotto and Heckler both published their own studies of pulicology, and they compared fleas of different and warring nationalities. Eastern European fleas were favoured over less robust specimens from the West. But then again we are still in scam land: a flea is still a flea, no matter what its passport says. Heckler was fond of saying, as he set up his circus, 'if a dog walks along now, my act's gone'.

So why did the fleas flee? A few bewitched souls are battling on with their tiny cart-pulling acts today, more in the pursuit of anthropology than viable entertainment, and God bless their brocade waistcoats. But the minuscule circus has largely gone the way of the adult circus and the music hall and all-in wrestling. The decline may be blamed on the modern world: better sanitation simply decreased the supply of decent performers. And the fleas that did survive gradually began to outnumber the audience. The amount of people prepared to part with a shilling to see a chariot move 4 inches along a flat board has – astonishing as it may seem – dwindled, and the shilling went instead to the cinema or the bookstore.

Chapter Four

The Miniature Book Society's Exciting Annual Convention

In the middle of August 2017, in an average-sized reception room at the Marriott City Center in Oakland, California, a man named Dr Arno Gschwendtner was selling, with a hint of pride, what he claimed to be the world's smallest book. It measured 0.7×0.7mm, and each of the twenty-two pages displayed both text and an illustration of a flower. If you placed it at the apex of your forefinger it resembled a speck of dirt.

The flowers in the book – and, it must be said, the text – all looked very similar, the cherry indistinguishable from the plum, but this wasn't really the issue: if you wanted a proper book about flowers you'd go to the Royal Horticultural Society or Robert Mapplethorpe. But if you wanted to read this book, which was published in Tokyo in 2013 with the title *Shiki no Kusabana*, you would have to use the little magnifying glass that accompanied it in a jewellery-style case lined with blue velvet (or you could read a larger version of the very same book, a book which Dr Gschwendtner called 'the mother', and which was also in the case, and measured a whopping just-under-an-inch square). Only 250 were made, and they were disappearing fast, so if you wanted to buy *Shiki no Kusabana* so that it could disappear while in your possession, now was the time to buy. Dr Gschwendtner wanted $750 for it.

Shiki no Kusabana was a stunt book. It was not just miniature, and not just microminiature, but ultra-microminiature. It was published by Toppan Printing Co., a Japanese publishing giant with its headquarters in a Tokyo skyscraper. Toppan has led the way in cutting-edge printing techniques since 1900, and every couple of decades it produced something previously considered impossible. To coincide with the New York World's Fair of 1965 it made a Bible 4×4mm, which it claimed was the smallest ever made. A few months later it outdid itself by publishing the poet Tu Fu's famous *The Eight Immortals of the Wine Cup*, in both Japanese and English, at only 3.75mm square. The height of each letter was about one-fifth the thickness of a human hair. There were special instructions on how to open the case in which the miniature book was housed.

But a few years later Toppan declared that 3.75mm was gargantuan. In 1979 it produced three new smallest books in the world, at 2×2mm. The books were exciting: *Calendar and Birth Stone*, *Language of Flowers* and *The Zodiacal Signs and their Symbols*. And then, with the birth of the digital world, these tiny books would be declared monstrous, and the 0.7×0.7mm flower book was unveiled.

The problem for Toppan was that it had competition from a Siberian named Vladimir Aniskin, whose hobby, when he wasn't working at the Russian Academy of Science in Tyumen, was making things on the split halves of poppy seeds. Before he turned to literature, Aniskin had made a nativity scene on a horse hair, and inscribed more than 2,000 letters on a grain of rice. And then, in 2016, came the news that Toppan's Japanese officials had been fearing: Aniskin had created two books measuring 0.07×0.09mm. This was 100 times smaller than anything Toppan had managed to make itself, and in the process had redefined the meaning of the word 'book'.

Clearly, Aniskin's creations weren't books in the popular sense of the word, and they couldn't be handled or their pages turned. They could be viewed only under a microscope, from where, Aniskin claimed, one could make out an alphabet (on the first book), and something he called Levsha (on the second). Levsha contained the names of other miniaturists who could 'shoe the flea', the ultimate microscopic challenge. (The feat was first described in the famous late-nineteenth-century fable 'The Tale of Cross-Eyed Lefty from Tula and the Steel Flea' by Nikolai Semyonovich Leskov. A Russian proves his skill by taking a 'clockwork steel flea' made by the English and giving each of its legs a horseshoe; the flea can no longer dance, and the value of the horseshoes is unclear, but Tsar Nicolas I is astounded, and that's good enough. The story appears to have been a plea to honour the handmade in the age of the machine, a message that all collectors of miniature books would approve.)

But just what is it with the Siberians? Between 1996 and 2012, before Vladimir Aniskin got to work, the smallest book was recognised as *Chameleon*, thirty pages at 0.9mm square, made by another Siberian, Anatoly Ivanovich Konenko. Konenko was another artist who could proudly shoe the flea, and much else besides: he could also make a grasshopper that played the violin on the upturned shell of a walnut, and, with his son Stanislav Konenko, a glass aquarium with miniature zebra fish that you could hold in the palm of your hand. Mr Konenko, who was born in 1954, has won thirty-six international awards for his tiny endeavours, including one for a 3.2mm-tall metal midge, which would have been just an ordinary micro midge had it not been for what it was displaying on its proboscis: a micro miniature Eiffel Tower.

A century before Siberia, the miniature book had an even less likely home – Grimsby. In 1891, the smallest book in the world was *The Mite*, published in this fishing port in northeast England at 13/16th of an inch high, with thirty-eight pages and twenty lines to the inch. Copies were bound in red leather and gilt, and its text, if you could read it, was unpredictable: there were stories about the invention of printing, the amount of steel used annually to make pins, and – because it was now so obviously a symbol of the modern scalable age – a brief history of the newly opened Eiffel Tower.

The battle to be the smallest for smallest sake began with the invention of movable metal type. Previously there were specific reasons for smallness: scribes would ink scriptures and psalms on tiny portions of uterine vellum, and religious men would secrete them about their person. Portions of the Bible and the Koran were popular for practical instruction and, as a token of devotion, concealed close to the heart. Before vellum there was the clay tablet: the earliest known examples from c.2300 BCE are trading contracts the size of a thumb.

After Gutenberg, the potential for portability expanded. When Aldus Manutius popularised italic type in Venice around 1500 (thus enabling more words on less paper), typesetters and printers attempted to outdo each other with minutiae. Very soon the books became collectable, and every library would have its miniature section. Tastes were eclectic: religious texts led the way, but by the end of the sixteenth century anything set in tiny text was popular.

The tradition continued. In 1961, the vast catalogue of one discriminating collector showed how varied the range had become; as varied, indeed, as the books produced at regular size. There were a great many almanacs with conversion tables, a large amount of ancient texts, a lot of lives of Christ, a few books on etiquette, and, more recently, good showings of Dickens, Swift and Milton. The books had one useful thing in common beyond their size: they were all out of copyright. (The collection was the property of an engineer named Percy Spielmann, who was one of the world's experts in road surfaces.)

Many of these titles are still available at reasonable prices. Indeed, of all the collectible arts, miniature books may be one of the most undervalued. In August 2017, an auction held by PBA Galleries in San Francisco contained a miniature edition of Cicero published in Paris in 1773; a book of *The Most Approved Sentimental English Songs* published in Baltimore in 1812; *The Rubáiyát of Omar Khayyám* made in Massachusetts in 1916; and *Extracts from the Autobiography of Calvin Coolidge* published in Tennessee in 1930. The hammer prices ranged from $150 to $850, and elsewhere in the sale there were further bargains: a complete set of Shakespeare's plays in forty volumes from 1930, each edition just over 2 inches tall, complete with their own tiny three-shelf bookcase, was sold for a mere $120. And modern collections – including fifteen books from the Somesuch Press in Dallas (once run by the late Stanley Marcus, the former president of the Neiman Marcus department store) – could be had for less.

A catalogue such as this may leave you with a few questions. The first may be: Is there any point to the miniaturisation of books beyond the challenge itself? And the follow-up may be: Were these volumes, at their core, fundamentally stupid?

To find out, I did two things: I paid $55 to join the Miniature Book Society (about 300 other members in 25 countries), and I attended the Miniature Book Society's 2017 annual summer convention at the Marriott in Oakland, California, which is where I first encountered the tiny offerings of Dr Arno Gschwendtner.

Dr Gschwendtner, a tall man of forty-three with brown curly hair and round Lennon-style glasses, had travelled to Oakland from Switzerland with a large selection of tiny books, almost all of which he could have concealed in the holes of a slice of Emmental. As well as perhaps the world's smallest, he also had one of the biggest: the Complete Sherlock Holmes collection, published in sixty volumes by Miniaturbuchverlag of Leipzig, about half of them available on Dr Gschwedtner's black baize table, each 53×38mm (about 2×1.5 inches), every word legible without the need for magnification, a steal at $20 per story. He also had beautiful modern versions of Edgar Allan Poe, Oscar Wilde, and (of course) *Gulliver's Travels* in four volumes. There were many older items too, including a copy of *De Flagrorum Usu in Re Veneria*, just over 3 inches by 2, which Dr Gschwendtner described as 'an exceedingly rare miniature edition of Johann Heinrich Meibom's famous book on the use of flagellation in medicine and sexual intercourse'. This was first published in Leyden, Holland, in 1629, although the doctor's edition was published in Paris in 1757, and came, reassuringly, 'tightly bound in mottled calf'.

Dr Gschwendtner grew up without a television at home, so reading has always been his thing. He had only been a doctor for about five years; before that he had worked as a waiter and a DJ, jobs he took solely to pay for his hobby. 'For about ten years I learnt all I could about miniature books – you can ask me anything you want,' he told me. I asked him about his smallest book, the book of flowers. He explained that Toppan did not make *Shiki no Kusabana* available for sale online, and so he flew to Tokyo expressly to buy several copies. 'It's completely crazy!' he said.

Like most scholars of the miniature book, Dr Gschwendtner had become an expert in minuscule typefaces. His copy of Jean de La Fontaine's *Fables* (Paris, 1850), for example, was printed in 2.5-point Diamant type from the foundry of Laurent et Deberny, a size about one-quarter of anything that may comfortably cross our eyes today, and 'much smaller than the English Diamond type used by Pickering'. Only thirty years before, when publisher William Pickering enlisted London printer Charles Corrall to print a series of miniature books in Diamond, a derivation of the famous Caslon typeface, it was the smallest then available at 4.5 point. And thirty years later, the type, carved from metal, went smaller still: in 1878, Dante's *La Divina Commedia* was printed in a size believed to be 2 point, and it was so small that it had its own nickname: Fly's Eyes. According to the 1911 catalogue of the miniature books in the library at the Grolier Club in New York, Fly's Eyes type 'injured the eyesight of both the compositor and corrector'. A century later, of course, microscopic texts would yield to the digital age. At Stanford in 1985, nanotechnologists reproduced the entire opening page of *A Tale of Two Cities* onto the head of a pin, reducing a regular 10-point typeface to 1/25,000th of its size. (It was the best of Times New Roman, it was the worst of Times New Roman.)

* * *

The Oakland Miniature Book Society convention called itself a conclave, which brought to mind papal secrecy and a distinct lack of roistering. The MBS conclave was meeting for the thirty-fifth year, and previous conclaves had been held in Dublin, Ottawa and New Orleans, with the very first attended by sixty-one people on a sweltering September day at a farm in Tipp City, Ohio, in 1983. The plan was to combine specialised academic bibliomania, bite-sized reading and gleeful collecting; like-minded souls could also convince themselves that being very interested in miniature books wasn't an entirely pointless or solitary pursuit. At the first conclave, the standard definable size of a miniature book was generally agreed to be anything up to 3 inches tall, although 4 inches was occasionally deemed acceptable. Five inches was simply too big, and 6 inches was almost a paperback.

Despite my misgivings, the Oakland conclave was jovial and celebratory, with trips to see the miniature collections at the Book Club of California, the San Francisco Public Library and several crafting workshops. It was not the youngest of gatherings, however, and there was an awareness that more had to be done to encourage younger people to join. One problem was, younger people already had all the 3-inch reading they could handle, and it was called a mobile phone.

Joining Dr Gschwendtner in the room at the Marriott were dealers from Scotland, the Netherlands and many parts of the United States. There were miniature books on cocktails and how to make them (1914), angling (1825), poems by Emily Dickinson (1997), and several editions of the complete works of Shakespeare. I was particularly attracted to a volume titled *Elevator Systems of the Eiffel Tower* by Robert M. Vogel, published by Plum Park Press at 3×2 inches and $45. And who wouldn't want, at 2.5×2 inches, one of thirty copies of the fully illustrated $150 edition of *Australian Quirky Letter Boxes*? After careful consideration I spent $25 on a hand-made book called *Autographs of Miniature Book Publishers*, published by the Tamazunchale Press in Newton, Iowa, in 1983. This contained a signature from all the publishers who had attended the first conclave, and it spoke of a thriving cottage industry 100 strong. Two of the signatures belonged to Anne Bromer and Julian Edison, who would later produce a classic pictorial history of their hobby – *Miniature Books: 4,000 Years of Tiny Treasures* – and sell at least one copy to everyone else in the autograph book. Amongst their treasures, Bromer and Edison include a book they call *Sophy's Album*, a 144-page bound manuscript measuring less than 2 inches in height in which an Englishwoman named Sophy Horsley collected autographs, sketches and musical compositions from her teenage years in the 1830s through to 1862. She had much help from the family friend Felix Mendelssohn, and between them they gathered brief notations from Brahms, Liszt, Paganini and Chopin, and additional contributions from Dickens and Sir Edwin Landseer. Bromer and Edison also highlight a miniature book that went to the Moon with Buzz Aldrin in Apollo 11 – an autobiography of Robert Hutchings Goddard, the pioneer of the liquid-propelled rocket.

Conclave attendees in Oakland were concerned not just

with content but also with art and paper engineering. There were several examples of books that fitted inside a walnut shell, for example, and many pop-up and illustrated children's books. A woman named Dorothy Yule, who, with her twin sister Susan, was the official host of the Oakland event, showed off an extraordinary multi-fold accordion of a book she had created for her husband's seventy-fifth birthday, containing a photo for every year of his life (her husband was Jim Parkinson, the type designer who created, amongst many other counterculture landmarks, the masthead-cum-logo for *Rolling Stone* magazine). Another autobiographical accordion-style work by Yule, describing her experiences as a young scientist, and containing several tiny pop-up illustrations of experiments in physics, chemistry and biology, was one of the most enchanting objects I had ever held. Yule's work in particular made me re-evaluate the worth of the miniature book: rather than just a reduced version of a standard text, the best of them had a quality that honoured the skill of the typesetter, printer and binder, and transported the reader to precious realms. A good miniature book managed, in the words of the fantasy writer and miniature book collector Ray Bradbury, to 'stuff your eyes with wonder'.

The highlight of the conclave was a gala dinner in the Marriott Skyline Room, where the miniature menu promised a pudding called caramel mystique. When that was eaten (it was crème brûlée), there were annual awards for the best handmade books and outstanding service to the society. I sat next to Caroline Brandt, who said she had been fascinated by miniature books since childhood, and, since she was now in her eighties, that meant there was little she didn't know about them. She told me she had attended every conclave since 1983, and had recently donated almost her entire collection (12,000 volumes, almost all under 3 inches) to the Albert and Shirley Small Special Collections Library at the University of Virginia, near her home. When she listed a number of famous miniature book collectors – including Mary Stuart, Empress Eugenie and Franklin Delano Roosevelt – there was one name I didn't recognise: Louis W. Bondy. She said that Bondy was a bookseller in London until his death in 1993, and was a great scholar of the miniature. She recalled his favourite phrase: 'My book is little, but my love is great.'

Brandt was also the author of her own miniature book, entitled *Many Littles Make a Much*. It contained several accounts of meetings with fellow enthusiasts, and one of these was a man named Achille 'Archie' J. St. Onge. Some of Brandt's details were a little vague. Archie was born in 1913 either in Canada or the United States, and he had a father who produced an uncertain number of children with four wives. Archie was brought up in an orphanage, and had a lazy eye, and drifted into publishing. He produced his first miniature book in 1935, and soon came to specialise in small volumes about Abraham Lincoln (he also published the book that Buzz Aldrin took to the Moon). His last miniature publication – of the forty-six he published to universal acclaim from the miniature book community – was an edition of *The Sermon on the Mount* from St Matthew's Gospel, and he commissioned a special binding for it from the London firm Sangorski & Sutcliffe. The book took four years to make, and it arrived at the home of Archie J. St. Onge two days after he died. 'Miniature books will never fail to delight,' Brandt said, 'and they will never fail to surprise you.'

'How much better than the Real Thing!': H. G. Wells (foreground, left)
and chums playing Little Wars in 1913.

Mini-break, 1911:
England's Playrooms

In 1911, the science fiction pioneer H.G. Wells published a short book explaining how and why he spent a good deal of his leisure time scrambling around on the floor on his knees, and it opened by considering what sort of floor was best. 'It must be a floor covered with linoleum or cork carpet, so that toy soldiers and such-like will stand upon it, and of a colour and surface that will take and show chalk marks.' There was one further instruction: 'It must be no highway to other rooms.'

Floor Games was a guide for children who wished to be taken seriously and for adults who felt childhood slipping away. It was a plea, in eighty-four illustrated pages, in those mythically innocent years before the world fell apart, for play that involved long-term strategy and instinctive tactics, much like computer games, much like war. The games included the building of cities and the defence of fortresses, and they were intended not merely for children to while away a few hours, but to construct 'a framework of spacious and inspiring ideas' for adulthood. The games, Wells hoped, would be the perfect prep for a career of governance: 'The British Empire will gain new strength from nursery floors.' (It was the same mindset that encouraged Wellington, albeit probably apocryphally, to suggest that the Battle of Waterloo was won on the playing fields of Eton.) In this case, Wells was fooling nobody: the games were primarily for him, and if his readers wanted to join in then good for them.

The main activity he proposed was called 'The Game of the Wonderful Islands', an adventure where the floor is the sea, and four islands are inhabited by soldiers, farmyard animals, camels, spear-carrying natives and all manner of tiny old effects representing an oppressive imperial history and glorious British future. Wells (and sometimes his children) move all these figures around the islands, along with guns and ships, and they divide and conquer until the evening descends. Occasionally there is burning, and sometimes there is cannibalism. In a time before irony or the guilt of empire, the author explains how 'we land and alter things, and build and rearrange, and hoist paper flags on pins, and subjugate populations, and confer all the blessings of civilisation upon these lands'.

Above all, then, Wells had a desire to control, and to explore the limits of what he believed was benign demagoguery. Sometimes this is expressed through his science fiction (the powerful invaders of *The War of the Worlds* (1898) are up on tripod stilts, towering over prey) and sometimes through semi-autobiographical novels such as *The New Machiavelli* (1911), in which the desires and impulses of his narrator Remington are informed primarily by the ability to control the world as if he were still a child. In the playroom, Remington ran 'an empire of the floor', in which towns and villages spread over an oilcloth, and the surrounding area consisted of 'water channels and open sea of that great continent of mind'. Everything is possible and pliable in miniature, the venue of fantasy, and too bad if the full-scale future disappoints.

Politically, as expressed through his essays, Wells was a philosopher of domination. He had visions for ideal communities and the social transformation of model cities, and his vision for a perfect world with perfect people tipped him towards eugenics; he considered, for example, how inbreeding may lead to the fostering of 'desirable types'. And of course the very nature of novel writing assumes a mastery of creation, a view from above that marshals both narrative and character. In *The Sleeper Awakes*, published just a year before *Floor Games*, Wells makes the view from above part of the story: the subject, who has awoken after centuries of sleep to find himself not only impossibly wealthy but also the ruler of a new London, takes to the air in a balloon and then an aeroplane to survey the tiny citizens below him. There is not much he can do to improve their downtrodden lives; only the novelist can determine their fate. Many years later, in his last major novel *The Shape of Things to Come* (1933), Wells envisages a protracted future encompassing the Second World War and a harsh and destructive 'Dictatorship of the Air' in which the old order is necessarily expunged to make way for the new utopia. Coming as it did in the shadow of global economic depression and the rise of the Third Reich, the optimism was rooted in a grim reality, the giant divine creator looking down as the earth convulses.

Back in the world of play, many of the items Wells required for his games and his cities, such as planks and boards, also reflected his omniscience: these were not things to be found by mere mortals in commercial toyshops. 'We do not, as a matter of fact, think very much of toyshops,' he wrote from the suburban playroom of his house in Kent. (By 'we' he chiefly means 'I'; his children were aged eight and ten at the time of publication, and if they possessed any negative thoughts about toyshops at all, it was probably only that they didn't live next door to one.) 'We think they trifle with great possibilities,' Wells continued. 'We consider them expensive and incompetent.' Wells especially repudiated the toyshops' supply of bricks. 'We see rich people, rich people out of motor cars, rich people beyond the dreams of avarice, going into toyshops and buying these skimpy, sickly, ridiculous pseu-do-boxes of bricklets, because they do not know what to ask for, and the toyshops are just the merciless mercenary enemies of youth and happiness . . .' The toyshops and their bricks were also to blame for the buildings inhabited by Wells's readers, for 'you see their consequences . . . in the weakly-conceived villas and silly suburbs that people have built all around London'.

By the time *Floor Games* was published, Wells was already truly famous, and the success of *The Time Machine*, *The Island of Doctor Moreau*, *The Invisible Man* and *The War of the Worlds* had provided a literary podium from which the author could write about anything he chose, and so he chose to follow up *Floor Games* with another short book named *Little Wars*. This too featured planks, bricks, toy soldiers and wallpaper-covered houses, and this time there were photographs of Wells engaged in the activities he described, both in the living room and on the lawn. One picture shows Wells with Jerome K. Jerome, who also enjoyed knocking down 2-inch Zulus with his spring-breech loader. Wells is wearing a boater, a blazer and white flannels, an image of the overgrown but under-developed Eton schoolboy, and it was from this lowly perch that Wells won himself a reputation as the Grandfather of Wargaming.

Everything that came after this image of the writer and his tin armies – every baized trestle table in the front room, every convention centre filled with malodorous men up since dawn to load their battlefield into the Astra and unpack it for their snippy peers – all owed something to Wells. Ultimately if indirectly, even the multibillion-dollar DVD and online games industry stemmed from Wells's plangent descriptions.

Wells claims forebears of his own. He suggests that an instinctive desire for one human to knock down the miniature army of another has existed as far back as humans and armies themselves. Games of Little Wars existed in prehistoric and ancient times, he states, and he himself had seen examples that existed at the time of Napoleon and Waterloo. Wells mentions the influential concept of 'kriegspiel', the nineteenth-century initiative developed by the Prussian and German armies to map and manoeuvre their forces on a gridded layout. Officers, dominant from above, moved troops according to dice and whim and the tactics of an opponent; the foot soldiers were tiny, and thus deemed disposable.

Little Wars was published in 1913, but the fragility of the world did not, at first, seem to bear any influence on the author's thinking. Only in his conclusion does Wells address the connection between the enjoyment to be gained from looming over tiny figures and the looming threat of genuine conflagration. 'How much better is this amiable miniature than the Real Thing!' he writes. The little lawn games he enjoys are containable and short-lived and purposefully happy; they end with domestic tea or tinned meat on a tablecloth. Little Wars is not, he suggests, merely Great War rendered smaller; it is, by its miniaturisation and manageability, a warning of what Great War is not. 'All of us, in every country, except a few dull-witted energetic bores, want to see the manhood of the world at something better than apeing the little lead toys our children buy in boxes,' Wells argues, insisting that his document of play should never be seen as an endorsement of barbarism; carpet-bombing should stay on the carpet. To this end he has one final Swiftian suggestion: let the game that mimics reality turn reality into the game. 'Let us put this prancing monarch and that silly scaremonger, and these excitable "patriots," and those adventurers, and all the practitioners of Welt Politik, into one vast Temple of War, with cork carpets everywhere, and plenty of little trees and little houses to knock down, and cities and fortresses, and unlimited soldiers – tons, cellars-full – and let them lead their own lives there away from us.'

Fat chance. Within a year, airships filled the skies. When one walked through central London in 1916 and viewed the devastation of the aerial bombing at street level, the blown-out fronts of private homes resembled nothing so much as doll's houses in open play.

The formal best of privileged England:
Queen Mary's Doll's House being packed
away in Edwin Lutyen's drawing
room in 1924.

Chapter Five

The Domestic Ideal

A visitor to Queen Mary's Doll's House at Windsor Castle may be charmed by many things. There is its size: 5 feet high and 8 feet 5 inches wide. There is its architectural importance: designed in the early 1920s by Sir Edwin Lutyens, it may be considered his most original creation; Lutyens was criticised for devoting more time to the model than he did to the full-scale building of the headquarters of the Anglo-Persian Oil Company. And then there is the fact that the Wren-style facade lifts up in its entirety to reveal something unique: a collection of elaborately furnished miniature rooms with hundreds of original paintings and antiques, and 700 tiny, readable books. Everything in the house is in fully working order, including electricity, water pipes and a lift shaft; the only thing not functioning is the telephone.

But who would be home to answer it? Of all the extraordinary things in the doll's house, one is struck, above all, by the fact that it has no dolls in it. It was never intended as a plaything, for it was always too precious to handle. Instead it was the embodiment, in one single space viewable (almost) all at once, of all that was finest about Britain as it limped

away from war. It contained such a high level of craftsman-
ship, and inspired in its creators such a forelock-tugging duty
to perform at the very peak of their abilities, that one may
reasonably claim that it has no fair comparison, in miniature
scale or any other.

Before the Great War, the traditional role of the miniature
house among European and Russian royal families had been
preservation. The doll's house served as a useful catalogue of
personal possessions, and doubled as a display of wealth. If
you fancied yourself as an interior decorator then it helped
with that too. But Queen Mary's house would go far beyond
this, crossing from the aspirational and merely perfectionist
into the greedy. It would contain not what the Queen already
owned, or perhaps once vaguely wished to own, but what she
couldn't possibly hope to acquire in this quantity at full scale.

It was the idea of Princess Marie Louise, a cousin of King
George V and a friend of the Queen since childhood. She
had observed the Queen's fascination with small things –
porcelain dishes, glass figurines, other trinkets – and was
perhaps aware of her reputation as a schnorrer: visiting friends
or public institutions, the Queen would frequently indicate
how much she liked a particular object, with a suggestion
(perhaps from her courtiers) that a gentle beheading may
ensue if it wasn't surrendered; accordingly, friends were known
to hide their most precious possessions before she called
round. In the spring of 1921, Princess Marie Louise wondered
whether she could persuade her friend Lutyens to create
something unique, and the architect saw it as an opportunity

for fun and favour (he was building much of New Delhi when the idea arose; he was most revered for his war memorial, the Cenotaph in Whitehall). Having accepted his miniature commission, Lutyens immediately went big, and declared it the grandest scheme: by the time he was done, 1,500 people would have been involved in its construction. He held court at the Savoy for what he called his 'Dollelujah dinners', at which he would discuss who should be commissioned and at what price; as well as a final list of 700 artists, there were some 500 donors who wished their names to be attached to the project, perhaps hoping for honour-favours in return.

There were a few easy early choices. Sir George Frampton, who would go on to design the sculpture of Peter Pan in Kensington Gardens, agreed to cast the ornamental facades, including the coats of arms; Cartier agreed to make a working longcase clock modelled on a seventeenth-century classic by Thomas Tompion; James Purdey & Sons Ltd signed up to make the sporting guns; Hardy Bros. Ltd made the three-piece Palakona split bamboo salmon fly rod; John Wisden and Co. Ltd made the willow cricket bat; and HMV made, after considerable ordeal, a fully workable fully scaled-down wind-up gramophone. The contents combined the weight of royal history (suits of armour, portraits of long-dead monarchs in the hallways) with the usual conveniences (the wooden commode chair by J. Bolding & Sons and the Chubb safe in the Queen's bedroom).

The greatest artists of the day from all technical and

cultural quarters were summoned to make something that could simply never be made again, and if they weren't immediately included in this summons, they would pull strings to be invited. The miniature house would be the Royal Academy, London Library, Harrods and all the skills of the great guilds distilled into one stacked domestic luxe utopia at a scale of 1:12. And that was only the bedrooms and public rooms. Other skills and services were required for the playroom (miniature model railway, tiny lead soldiers); kitchen (copper pans made from gold, marmalade from Frank Cooper and Colman's mustard on the oak table); larder (tiny jars of Chivers strawberry jam and tins of Rowntree's Clear Gums); and wine cellar (more than 200 bottles of wine from Berry Bros., sealed with wax, alongside Gilbey's gin and Louis Roederer champagne). In the rooms above, servants' quarters had bedpans beneath sprung mattresses and fires in the grates; below, a Rolls-Royce Silver Ghost lay purring on the herringboned drive.

Then – and why not? – there was a garden designed by Gertrude Jekyll, who was almost blind by the time she took up her miniature hoe. And of course there was a workable miniature globe in the library, and sheets of Bromo lavatory paper by the wooden toilet seats and Vim by the sinks, and sash windows that worked with a system of weights in the traditional way. And why wouldn't the Silver Ghost have a tiny silver-tipped whisky flask set into a door?

By now one is not surprised to learn that the Trunk Room and Linen Room were both extensively stocked. (The linen, the writer Lucinda Lambton has observed, consists of damask, cotton, flannel and wool, and every item, from the towels in the servants' quarters to the pillowcases in royal bedchambers, have been monogrammed with such delicacy 'that one is tempted to say it could only have been the work of fairies'; it turns out to be the work of a lone Irish French seamstress, and it took her 1,500 hours.) But the grandest room is the Library, and the most impressive thing of all is that the vast majority of the books are shelved with only the spines visible. You would expect this of a full-size library, where each volume may be opened and examined by all, but not perhaps in a library where a newly illustrated version of *If* by Rudyard Kipling and a freshly hinged Stanley Gibbons stamp album, not to say a small composition from Gustav Holst, are viewable only to the present owner of the Queen's doll's house, who, at the time of writing, turns out to be the Queen.

One of the items she can enjoy is a miniature (twenty-four-page) Sherlock Holmes story written especially for the library by Sir Arthur Conan Doyle, entitled *How Watson Learned the Trick*. But she may prefer Robert Graves, who contributed five new handwritten poems, two fewer than Thomas Hardy; or verse from Edith Wharton, A.E. Housman, Aldous Huxley and Siegfried Sassoon. Ernest Shepard, the illustrator of *Winnie the Pooh*, designed the 'ex libris' bookplates attached to each volume, a woodcut of Windsor Castle below the initials M.R. (for Mary Regina). Tiny art came in from Paul Nash, Laura Knight, H.M. Bateman, Arthur Rackham, W. Heath Robinson, William Nicholson, Helen Allingham,

Edmund Dulac, George Gilbert Scott, C.R.W. Nevinson and Mark Gertler. Special library cabinets were constructed to house all the paintings and illustrations for which the walls had no space. There were about 700 of them.

A few dissenters declined to join the party. Virginia Woolf and George Bernard Shaw both sent their apologies, but the least apologetic was Elgar. Writing in his diary, the poet Siegfried Sassoon recalled the composer saying

> We all know that the King and Queen are incapable of appreciating anything artistic. They've never asked for the full score of my Second Symphony to be added to the Library at Windsor . . . But I'm asked to contribute to a Doll's House for the Queen! . . . I consider it an insult for an artist to be asked to mix himself up in such nonsense.

The doll's house is absurd and fantastical, but it is not nonsense. After a while, though, I imagine even Lutyens and his assistants must have tired of the detail of the acquisitions. And perhaps they began to wonder whether there was anything that couldn't be convincingly miniaturised. Or was there anything, once it had been convincingly miniaturised, that would fail to fascinate and amuse for generations to come?

* * *

One traipses up the hill from one of the car parks in the town, past the Pizza Express and the man offering free samples at the fudge shop, and all the guides on the edge of Windsor Castle are in uniform. Admission is more than £20, and there's a queue at the box office and an even longer one before you're admitted to the doll's house at the edge of a relatively new part of the castle, which means it was only built around the time of Henry VIII in the sixteenth century (the old bit goes back almost to the Norman invasion).

The doll's house has been on public display since 1924, first at the British Empire Exhibition at Wembley for seven months, then for a few more at the Ideal Home Exhibition, and ever since (with the exception of a period of restoration at the V & A and Science Museum in the mid-1970s) at Windsor Castle. When the little house was finished, Queen Mary sent Lutyens a modest token of her appreciation: a letter of thanks and a signed photograph.

Today the doll's house is encased in a tall and toughened sheet-glass box, of the type that might otherwise contain Hannibal Lecter, and my own experience of looking at it was not enhanced by an unappeasable steward who encouraged everyone not to dawdle, but to move around all four sides of the house as quickly as possible because the queue outside was long and getting longer. It was as if we had stumbled across a crime scene to be told there was nothing to see here. At one point he actually said, in what should have been *sotto voce* but was actually a boom, 'You ask them to move along and do they listen?'

Even with the glass and the verbal pressure, the delight in seeing the doll's house today has not diminished. The shell of the house is forever fully suspended over its innards, and, unlike most conventional face-on doll's houses, one views the model in the round. The external and internal lighting both project an air of continual twilight: it would be bedtime for the children, so the toys are half put away; but it would be cocktail and dressing-up hour for the adults, so the tables are set and there is an air of expectation. Almost a century on, the house is not outmoded; it has become simply more exceptional. One needs no particular taste to appreciate it, nor any learned judgement: one needs merely enough breath to gasp 'a tiny Hoover with wound electric flex and half-full dust bag in the housemaid's closet! A Shell petrol pump in the garage with rubber tubing!' Perfection is ingrained in every detail, and, at an inch to the foot, the detail reflects the formal best of privileged England. Its creators could not possibly have guessed how soon it would come to represent the end of it.

It would be very difficult, if one were aged between four and ten, and perhaps also a girl, to visit Queen Mary's Doll's House and not immediately want one for oneself. So observed the essayist A.C. Benson, and it is true, if quaint: a girl with even the wealthiest of parents would struggle to come even close to it in either extent or execution. But one who came close in her own way was a woman named Narcissa Niblack Thorne, who read about Queen Mary's gift in the magazines, and in 1932 began work on what would become a comparable marvel – a set of sixty-eight individual miniature rooms that traced the development of European and American homes from Gothic thirteenth-century France to 1940s Californian modern. The rooms were made primarily to the familiar scale of 1:12, and as a magnificent depiction of the development of interior decoration they stand alone.

Born Narcissa Niblack in Indiana in 1882, Mrs Thorne was the daughter of a distinguished and much-travelled businessman, and by the time she moved to Chicago around 1900 she had already seen much of Europe and America. Her wealth and social connections increased with her marriage at the age of nineteen to James Ward Thorne, and she became a generous host and patron of the arts. She had collected miniatures from a young age – furniture, pictures, other household objects – but in the 1920s her hobby found a new direction. She was fascinated by the period rooms she saw in museums, and wondered whether, by using her own collection and commissioning new pieces, she could form a visually arresting room display in miniature. Her modest ambitions soon overtook her, and what began as a slightly scattershot array of period furniture swiftly became a principled devotion. She would, she resolved, depict a personal history of domestic living, or at least its upper echelons, in a comprehensive and painstakingly accurate way. Her son recalled how his mother once had thirty individual rooms in her studio in various stages of completion, attended also by experts in mouldings and flooring. Large queues formed when her first rooms went on show in 1932 at the Chicago Historical Society, and visitors have flocked ever since.

One may see Narcissa Thorne's work today in a permanent exhibition occupying a narrow walkway on the lower ground floor of the Art Institute of Chicago, and it takes one's breath away. The framed, lit boxes are precisely proportioned and engrossing, but above all they are beautiful, and one hesitates only briefly before calling them magical. We peer into secret worlds, but recognise them at once, for they are the worlds of glossy magazines and movies.

There are twenty-nine European rooms, all but one of them English or French (the exception is German, a Biedermeier-period sitting room from the early nineteenth century). Just one example from England – a marble-floored drawing room from the 1930s from which the open French windows give way to Regent's Park – may be sufficient to measure the care placed upon the construction of them all. The dove-grey walls have elaborate rococo plasterwork, Chippendale chairs mix with a chromium and glass table set with cocktail shaker and cigarette case, and a newspaper lies ruffled on a simple modern couch. It is elegant, airy and restrained, and one can almost smell the white lilies in the blue vase. And all within a fairly typical 17×27×21 inches. It was a room that required none of the research needed, say, for the Queen Anne Cottage Kitchen or the Georgian

Entrance Hall, for it was a drawing room in which Mrs Thorne herself would have flounced with Cecil Beaton. As at Windsor, only a war could shatter its confidence.

The thirty-seven American rooms range from a Massachusetts living room and kitchen circa 1675 to the 1940s Californian dream, and en route takes in drawing rooms and parlours from Cape Cod to New Mexico. In the last room, the future beckons: the West Coast Hallway features original work from Fernand Léger and others, while the view beyond is the Golden Gate Bridge. The only concession to the East comes with a traditional, and thus undated, *zashiki* interior from Japan, all sliding panels and lacquer desk and harmonious bamboo. But every Thorne room is ultimately harmonious, for this is an attribute we have already judged to be consistent with every exquisite miniature. A tiny object in proportion calmly beguiles us like no other.

If you can't make it to Chicago, try the digital trail online. This 'Game of Thornes' is a clue-led maze, each accurate cursor click on a computer screen taking the player to another clue or another room. The object of the game, which may come across as both claustrophobic and undermining, is to gather enough information to 'escape from this mystifying realm of riddled rooms'. One clicks on the bed in the late-sixteenth-century French bedroom, for example, and reads that the underside of its canopy has an embroidered message urging us to find three letters to hasten our escape. Passing through the door, one is transported to the French boudoir of the mid-1750s, and if one clicks on a white marble sculpture near the fireplace one reveals the letter 'M'.

Too bored to click on, I decided to walk to the one example of Mrs Thorne's work on show in London. This is from 1936, when she received an unexpected but pleasingly circuitous commission – a request from the royal family to build a model of the library at Windsor Castle to honour the (soon-to-be-abandoned) coronation of Edward VIII. This now resides at London's V & A. It couldn't compete with Queen Mary's Doll's House, of course: swell as it is, the hundreds of books on its shelves can be neither opened nor read.

As with Queen Mary's Doll's House, none of the Thorne rooms make any allowance for dolls. To do so would have obscured pieces of furniture, and lessened our ability to imagine our own selves draped upon them. But there is another reason: dolls do not really look like miniature people. We are sinuous and over-animate; a doll is too easy to read. Observing a nativity scene, which we may regard as the precursor to the doll's house, we seldom feel the need to exclaim 'Those Wise Men – uncanny!' To have placed dolls within the exquisite objects at Windsor or Chicago would have made those big glass eyes and chiffon dresses and horse-hair hair seem even more artificial; the only things some dolls may be miniatures of are larger dolls.

But dolls – male and female, realistic and less so – may have other uses within a miniature landscape. They may, in their lifelessness, come to represent a darker side of human behaviour, and there can be no better example of this than in the work of Frances Glessner Lee.

In her younger days, Lee used to decorate regular doll's houses in the regular manner – that is, with meticulous precision. She created other charming models too, such as the entire Chicago Symphony Orchestra: ninety musicians with ninety instruments. But she will be remembered for something more unnerving, and more useful. Ms Lee was born four years before Mrs Thorne, and they both lived in Chicago, and they died in their mid-eighties. Their private passions suggest they could have been born in the same house, but – to borrow from Truman Capote – Thorne went out the front door, while Lee went out the back.

In the 1940s Frances Glessner Lee perfected small-scale but realistic box models depicting places where something terrible had happened. The models are made from wood, cloth, metal, plastic and glass, and from all the other materials one might expect to find in a commonplace home, and nineteen of them survive, though there may have been others that failed to reach completion. The models each took several months to construct, and all have accurate and potent period details; she was convinced that had she got her details wrong, or constructed an object shoddily, she would have swiftly lost her viewers' attention. Accordingly, the rugs on the floor, the soaps by the sink, the bread on the table and the mirrors on the wall are all perfect miniaturisations. A coffee percolator contains real grounds, a bathroom has a very small bottle of medicine to hand, while an armchair in a living room is chintzy and comfortable enough to make the viewer feel they may almost want to be sitting there.

But not quite: the rooms also contain representations of people bloodied on the kitchen floor, and hanging from a rope, and collapsed at the bottom of the stairs. A body slumped backwards in a bath has water gushing on its face from an open tap. Sometimes the rooms show signs of devastation and struggle, but at other times there's just lipstick on a pillow. But there would always be a corpse, for murder was Frances Glessner Lee's business, and the corpse would always be properly turned out – tights under bloomers under a skirt, knitted slippers with genuine leather soles – a recognisable life created only to snuff it out. Lee called her models the Nutshell Studies of Unexplained Death, and, some eighty years after they were created, a few of them remain unexplained.

Lee's passage from the genteel to the gory was inspired by a friend named George Burgess Magrath, a Boston medical examiner who was often appalled at the cavalier behaviour of police officers at a crime scene before he became involved in the case (they would move or remove evidence, they would clean up the blood). Lee's tableaux were imaginary, although often based on Magrath's accounts or murder reports in the newspapers. Her added touches – the mouth-watering contents of a tray in a cooker, the fresh sheets billowing on a clothes line – were designed as purposeful bait. These enticing objects may or may not lead the viewer to find a motive, a method and a murderer (although not every corpse had encountered foul play: there was the odd accident and natural cause in there too). Above all, Lee intended her dioramas to be educational, an aid to observation at a scale of roughly one inch to one foot (1:12). A 30-inch table came down to just under 3 inches, while a revolver of about 11 inches would be reduced to an inch. The intention, she said, was to start at the top of each model and observe the contents in an inwardly swirling clockwise motion, progressing slowly to ensure nothing would be missed, and ending with the body at the centre; ninety minutes should be sufficient to gather all the clues. She regarded her work not as art or craft, and certainly not as entertainment (but it was a neat thing that her models were roughly the size of an early television set). Her work had none of the aesthetic attraction of the Thorne rooms. Rather, Lee thought of her work as science, and she would have been delighted that her experiments are still of value today.

*   *   *

Whenever her name appeared in the newspapers, which, in later life, happened with frequency, Frances Glessner Lee was invariably referred to as 'a wealthy grandmother'. That she was, but if the description conjures an image of the society matron, one should think again. Before she became a crime modeller, Frances Glessner Lee was a justice fanatic. Partly perhaps to safeguard her own position of privilege, but also to protect the vulnerable, she did whatever she could to enhance police practice and efficiency. Above all, she believed in the purposeful and uncorrupted crime-fighter's mission to 'convict the guilty, clear the innocent, and find the truth in a nutshell'. To this end, in the early 1930s she helped establish the Harvard Department of Legal Medicine and the Harvard Associates in Police Science, both designed to modernise homicide investigation: scientific techniques of deduction, rather than traditional investigation methods or blunt instinct should now lead the way, she believed, and her belief was revolutionary. The annals call her the mother of forensics, and her focus, and those she influenced, may have saved untold numbers from execution. Her bloody dioramas were an extension of this process: by reducing an act to its key components she enabled viewers to see what really mattered. Even today, when we are fully educated in scepticism, it is difficult to look at the models and not feel a combination of revulsion and admiration. They're but boxes of play, but they work an unfeasible trick: they cloud us with doubt, and doubt foreshadows enquiry.

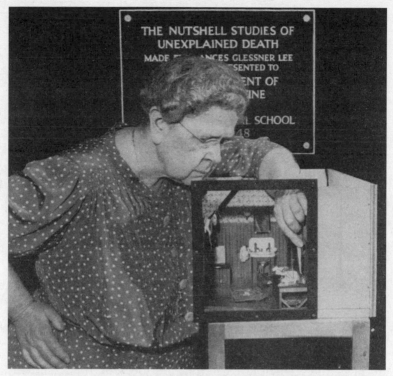

Her bloody dioramas: Frances Glessner Lee tweezering
a Nutshell Study in 1949.

Lee knew death well. Between 1929 and 1936 she lost
her brother, mother, daughter and father. As Corinne May
Botz observes in her book of close-up photographs of Lee's
models, Lee may be regarded as a study in consolation. She
was stern, strident and caustic, with one family member
describing her as a wonderful case for a psychiatrist. She
looked manly: short hair, no make-up, prominent features,

wire-rim glasses; even the most junior psychologist would have noted a desire to fit into a male-dominated world. Her early life, according to Botz, was both sheltered and suppressed, and her comfortable upper-class background was accompanied by limited paternalistic expectations. She mastered domestic handiwork while her professional horizons narrowed; her requests to attend Harvard were deemed unladylike. Lee schemed to escape her oppressive parents; her three children from a dissolved marriage reported her happiest only when she had flown from their clutches. Her fortunes changed markedly in the 1930s with her first contact with George Magrath, and her first taste of financial independence.

Lee loved both Sherlock Holmes and Agatha Christie, and perhaps it was not entirely coincidental that her appearance came to resemble Christie's Miss Marple, all hair bun and strict demeanour in dark, high-buttoned blouses and a hat influenced by the style worn in the 1920s by Queen Mary. But she knew more than anyone how appearances may deceive. She was not interested in the social high life featured in many of Christie's warming reads, but instead championed the underclasses; many of Lee's boxes reflected the uncertainties and indignities of harsh urban living. Although daily struggle could not in itself explain the terrible ends visited upon the dolls in her boxes – in a bedsit, a barn, a porch, a garage – it did root them in grim realism; a sense of overwhelming sadness pervaded many of her scenes.

The large majority of her victims were women, but their miniature demise was witnessed exclusively by men. 'The inspector may best examine them by imagining himself a trifle less than six inches tall,' she explained. 'A few moments of observation will then make him able to step into the scene and there find many tiny details that might otherwise escape notice.' She claimed her models aimed to depict each scene at its most 'effective' moment, 'very much as if a motion picture were stopped at such a point'.

Lee's models are each accompanied by a few paragraphs of text. These are from 'witnesses', often family members or local acquaintances of the deceased who discovered the bodies and thus provided important testimony, albeit imaginary. At the scene of 'The Pink Bathroom', for example, which features 'Mrs Rose Fishman' dead on the floor, the witness was Samuel Wiess, her janitor. 'Several tenants complained of an odor,' he recalled in his statement, 'and on March 30th I began looking for what was causing the smell.' Obviously he smelt Fishman. She didn't answer the doorbell, and when Wiess looked through her letterbox he saw an accumulation of mail. He entered the premises, tried unsuccessfully to open the bathroom door, so used the fire escape to climb in through the bathroom window and found Mrs Fishman slumped.

'It must not be overlooked,' Mrs Lee subsequently explained, 'that these statements may be true, mistaken, or intentionally false, or a combination of any two or three of these. The observer must therefore view each case with an entirely open mind.' In the case of Mr Wiess, his statement was true. Mrs Fishman had hung herself from her bathroom door, but only the keenest of eyes would have noticed a few threads of the blue cord from her bathrobe still present at the top of it; Wiess had dislodged her suspended body as he tried to force entry.

The scene in 'The Pink Bathroom' was quite different from the one in 'Dark Bathroom', the one with the body in the bath with the gushing tap. The body here was Maggie Wilson, the witness her roommate Lizzie Miller. Miller stated on oath that Wilson was prone to seizures (one possible cause), but also that the night she discovered her body she had been visited in her room by two men, and there had apparently been a lot of drinking (another). Was the water intended to drown the victim or revive her after a fit? Was the body moved after rigor mortis set in, and why was it in such an awkward position? What did the bottle on the rug and the nearby medications suggest? The creator of the puzzle – the woman who knitted the deceased's black cotton stockings with needles the size of pins and then wrote to her son about the ridiculous arduousness of the task – had succeeded in drawing us away from the intricate size of her model into a far bigger world.

Some eighty years later we are still captivated by Lee's work. The uniqueness of her models has, over the decades, inevitably been enhanced by quaintness, but they remain far from picturesque. In the autumn of 2017 they were the subject of an exhibition at the Smithsonian, but they usually reside close by on an upper floor of the Office of the Chief Medical Examiner in Baltimore. (The OCME also hosts the annual Frances Glessner Lee Seminar in Homicide Investigation, attended by detectives and pathologists and lawyers, and a few hours peering in and over the Nutshells are an integral part of the week-long event.) Her work has inspired fiction, and a season of the television series *CSI: Crime Scene Investigation* featured the Miniature Killer, a serial murderer who left her own intricate catch-me-if-you-can scale models at the scene of her slayings. Lee would have deplored her crimes, but she would have adored her attention to detail.

What one is left with, after looking at these models from all angles and in every age, is an unmistakable sense of an ambition realised. Whether or not you solve the mystery of the body in the pink bathroom is not the point, and never has been. The point is, Lee had harnessed the full potential of the miniature, and it is the same potential that linked all the rooms in Queen Mary's Doll's House and the work of Narcissa Niblack Thorne. The closer one looks, the more one sees, the closer one looks.

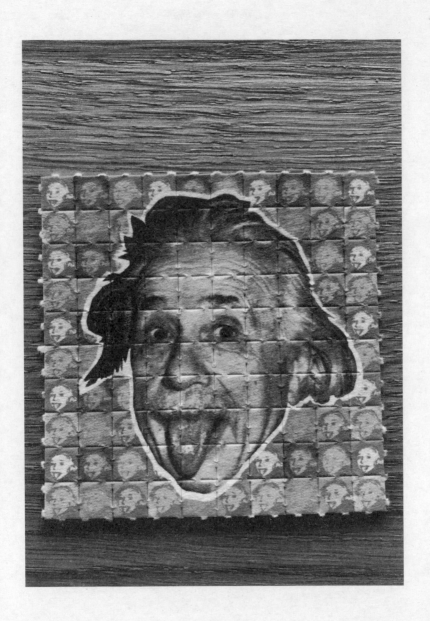

Mini-break, 1967:
San Francisco's Greatest Hits

Fifty years after the birth of the Summer of Love, the Mission District has not quite gone the way of the rest of San Francisco. It's a still place. The digital world has left this part of town alone, so you can still find cheap burritos and thrift stores, and you can probably still score and get mugged. And you will still find Mark McCloud holed up here behind permanently drawn curtains and a sign on his door that says 'I'm still voting for Zappa'.

McCloud is an artist of the acid scene. He has also become its accidental archivist. The walls of his living room are covered with framed blotter art, an enchanting by-product of the delivery system of LSD. Many of the artefacts measure 7.5 inches square, just larger than the sleeve of a vinyl single, and their images reflect the trippy counterculture – intergalactic explosions, mystic symbols, Robert Crumb characters – and the sort of multicoloured visions one might experience while hallucinating. A closer look reveals that they are not one whole unbroken image, but a perforated sheet of 900 or 1,000 tabs. Their chemical potency has long since evaporated, and they are no longer able to send you to another planet.

But their miniature artistic value remains, and it has fallen upon Mark McCloud's shoulders to protect it.

I had arranged to meet him one afternoon in August 2017. There was no answer when I rang his bell and banged on his door, and when I phoned him the following day he offered an undeniable explanation for his absence: 'Sometimes I'm in, and sometimes I'm out.' On my next visit he was wearing a black T-shirt emblazoned with skulls and there were already other fans in the room: a couple of stoners from Texas who found it difficult to get up from his sofa. McCloud held forth on a throne-like chair beneath a mantelpiece with three clocks, two of them modelled on melting timepieces by Salvador Dalí. Behind him was a large photograph of Albert Hoffman, the Swiss chemist who took a psychedelic bicycle ride back from his lab after first synthesising and sampling LSD in 1943. When my wife called on McCloud again a few days later to obtain a copy of a sheet, he traded his artwork for a loaf of her freshly baked sourdough. 'I love bread,' he explained. 'The only thing I don't like is couscous.' He said he'd experienced a bad couscous/acid event in Paris, although the details remained vague.

McCloud grew up in Argentina. His mother, from Oklahoma, was of Cherokee descent, while his father, a welterweight boxing champion, was from California; they moved to South America when his father got a job assembling military vehicles after the Second World War. McCloud remembers a solitary childhood collecting stamps and the items that came with packs of gum. His first miniature odyssey featured ants. 'I had eight on my ant farm and they all had different personalities and names.' He also had a coin collection, and he photographed his ants 'modelling' on pesos.

The family moved back to California in 1966, and McCloud says he first took acid in Santa Barbara a year or so afterwards, when he was in his early teens. He fell in love with Aldous Huxley and the Grateful Dead, and his art degree and drug taking jointly enhanced his appreciation of psychedelic design. In the mid-'70s he noticed that the tiny illustrations on his hits were becoming increasingly imaginative. 'The numismatist and philatelist in me took over,' he says (a phrase perhaps never previously uttered by an acid head), 'and so I started collecting seriously. I admired the fact that one could capture so much beauty on such a tiny surface, and that they could be *useful*.' He decided they were worth preserving, and his Institute of Illegal Images was born. 'The little old framer guy I used up at Noe Valley had no idea what they were,' he says. 'I came to pick up an order one day and he was closed, and I thought, "Oh no, he's licked his fingers and I've killed him."'

Like all good museums, there's a shop. McCloud sells giant art print enlargements of his most iconic images for $1,000, including *The Mighty Quinn* (an Eskimo looking out to sea), a cool Snoopy in sunglasses (boasting what McCloud calls 'an illegal smile'), and *The Sorcerer's Apprentice* (thought to have been dosed with LSD from Albert Hofmann's own laboratory). He has also licensed for sale a miniature book called *Blotter Barn Hits*, 2 inches square, showing similar classics: unicorns, golden keys, the rings of Saturn, an image of Mikhail Gorbachev ('the Gorby that brought down the Berlin Wall'). Even as acid-free reproductions they are entrancing things, their power enhanced by their size.

Before it was criminalised in the mid-1960s, psychoanalysts and hippies could get their acid in various ways. Large pills were popular, as were dipped lengths of string and sugar cubes. But when concealment and transportation became an issue, and the drug became increasingly commercialised, dealers looked for easier ways to distribute their wares. Jail terms for possession were based initially on the weight of the delivery method rather than the strength of dosage, so experiments were made with infused gelatin. But nothing proved as effective or transportable as thick absorbent paper.

Initially, doses were dropped individually onto litmus paper; the usual distribution was 5×20 drops on a rectangular sheet, with each blue dot then cut up for consumption. Standard blotting paper soon took its place, with whole sheets dipped and then broken up. Perforations swiftly removed the need for scissors. The tabs were technology; the smallest and most efficiently distributed method of bringing a desirable product to a mass market. Commercial art had suddenly shrunk to something smaller than a fingernail, or a SIM card, or an emoji.

Even users without heightened powers of perception soon began to notice that their individual hits had little motifs on them. They served a dual purpose: they signified the strength of the dose, and they signified the doser. It was branding for hippies: proud LSD labs wished to establish their credentials as drug makers you could trust, and visual artists who had made a big thing about dropping out found an authentic way to drop back in.

My introduction to blotter art came not from McCloud, but years before from a man named Lucifer. Lucifer was a thirty-one-year-old former traveller residing in a converted dairy farm near Horsham in the Sussex countryside, and he told me Lucifer was his birth name. He both collected and designed, and he was a former user. Viewing his collection was like a mild trip in itself. He showed me the first sheet he had seen in its entirety, a complex design featuring Timothy Leary in profile. A skull and crossbones sat on Leary's shoulder, musical notes emerged from his ear, and his teachings – something called 'Space Migration equals Intelligent Life Extension' or SMILE – lay alongside. 'I think it was 1995, and I was at a rave site before the rave had started. There was a sofa around a fire, and I sat on that and someone turned up with a new sheet that had just been dipped and it was this one. People held it and went, "Wow!" You could feel the energy from it through your fingertips.'

He remembers that parts of certain sheets were stronger

than others. Sometimes they were held up by a top corner after the dipping, so that the LSD would drip to the bottom. 'On the Timothy Leary I was told that the sheet was dipped again just on the skull and crossbones.' He says he stopped using LSD in his early twenties, citing safety issues. 'Every person that touches a dipped sheet adds their energy to it. I had taken various ones that had led me to negative perceptions . . . I was almost experiencing someone else's life history.' He reaches for his plastic folders. 'This is *The Simpsons*,' he says. 'And this is a *Beavis and Butt-Head*, and the Hendrix, and *Easy Rider*, and the *Dancing Skeletons*.' Lucifer told me that if I thought that his collection was impressive, I really hadn't seen anything at all. The collector to beat, he said (while adding that beating him was impossible), was a man who lived in San Francisco named Mark McCloud.

McCloud has his own hero, a man named Forester. Forester was a local blotter artist who couldn't resist his wares, and when he was busted for distribution and sent to San Quentin for ten years in 1988, McCloud took over his design duties, cementing his switch from collector and cheerleader to creator and player. McCloud's most famous work appeared in 1993 – the 900-hit *Alice Through the Looking Glass*, the perfect collision of image and substance. This appeared in various colours and strengths, but all had the same image of Alice stepping through a mirror into strange and unpredictable adventures. The White Rabbit, the Cheshire Cat and Humpty Dumpty look on, while text from Lewis Carroll's 'Jabberwocky' fills the remaining space. That's one side. On the other she emerges through the mirror with trepidation. The illustrations lean heavily on the nineteenth-century drawings by Sir John Tenniel, although McCloud also credits his design to a memorable trip taken shortly after he was busted by the Drug Enforcement Administration (an investigation codenamed Operation Looking Glass).

McCloud beat the rap, and repeated the trick a decade later in 2003. For the second trial, the DEA seized and analysed thousands of sheets from McCloud's home (he claims the figure was 33,000), and prosecutors argued that with so much blotter in his possession McCloud must be distributing. McCloud reasoned that it was easy to misinterpret his miniature collection; he said he was no more guilty of dealing than a tobacconist selling Rizla papers. Not, of course, that he hadn't consumed that which he collected. In his second court case he told the jury of his psychedelic rebirth when, in the early 1970s, he fell to what he described as his near-inevitable death through a high window. He was saved and abetted, he explained, by the muscle-relaxing and mind-expanding properties of a particularly fantastic tab of Orange Sunshine. The jury believed him, and they believed him again when he told them he was now a curator. 'They loved all the exhibits,' McCloud remembered. 'They just couldn't get enough of them.'

When his 2003 trial was over, McCloud found that his obscure hobby had become part of a buoyant market. There has yet to be an official catalogue establishing blotter rarity and pricing, and collectors have yet to be embraced by a major auction house. But if the market does ever take off, perhaps with interest from Russia or the Far East, McCloud will find himself a multimillionaire. His collection possessed one element guaranteeing future rarity: no matter how treasured its new-found value as art, a haul of blotter would forever be competing against someone's need to freak out.

These days eBay has a huge range of reproduction sheets on offer, and most are available for the cost of blotting paper in a stationer's shop. But occasionally a sheet goes for thousands. One example, called *60 Years of LSD – Mindstates IV*, had a 'Buy It Now' price of £2,750. Surely this was drenched in drugs. In fact, the price was due to the signature, at the foot of the sheet, of Albert Hoffman. (Hofmann died in 2008 aged 102.) The listing claimed that £2,750 would buy you 'A Holy Grail of Blotter Art . . . the pinnacle of most blotter collections. Not many people can boast a Hoffman. It comes with a photocopied letter by Dr Hoffman but don't ask me what it says as it is not in English.' The listing ended with a warning to those hoping for something illegal and transformative: 'These sheets are Artworks and only Artworks. They are intended for enjoyment of the art and nothing else. To suggest they are anything else or intended for any other reason, other than being works of art, is simply hearsay.' So yes, they were definitely drugs.

Impressive and deranged: visitors at Miniatur Wunderland ponder
the view from Rome.

Chapter Six

The Biggest Model Railway in the World

'If someone came into your home and said that for no charge he would run a Lionel model train . . . all around the inside perimeter of your house, a quiet train that makes a gentle choo-choo cooing here and there and that might blow little puffs of smoke and that would run all the time (as demonstrators do in model train shops, perhaps you've seen these), would you tell him no or would you tell him to knock himself out and lay that Lionel down?'

(From *The Interrogative Mood* by Padgett Powell)

In the port city of Hamburg a new settlement has sprung up called Miniatur Wunderland. This is the biggest model railway in the world, with a track length of almost 16,000 metres. Since nailing down its first rails in 2000, more than 15 million people have come to marvel at the expansive layouts. The writer George R.R. '*Game of Thrones*' Martin and the boxer Wladimir 'I'll knock your head off!' Klitschko have both been in, as have a great many German comedians and politicians (their photos hang on the wall by the entrance). Visitors have arrived from all over the world, including, by early October 2017, 129,444 from the UK, 83,212 from the USA, 57,318 from China and 59 from Burkina Faso. No fewer than 1,441,002 have popped in from Schleswig-Holstein. Some of the visitors have returned many times, and feel so at home in Miniatur Wunderland that they call it 'MiWuLa'. Just to be clear: 16,000 metres of track is roughly 10 miles.

The fact that Miniatur Wunderland is in Hamburg, in northern Germany, is not, I imagine, hugely significant to most of those who visit, but it is to me. My father was born here, and my grandparents too. My grandparents were married in a grand hotel overlooking the Elbe, which flows directly beneath the building housing the model railway. The Elbe is one of the few old things here, for much of the city was destroyed by the Allies in the war, by which time my father was a lance corporal in England. So a whole new Hamburg has been created in this city, both at full scale and in miniature. But the ambitious people who built the miniature version thought their train shouldn't just stop in Germany, so their track layouts have grown to incorporate Austria, Switzerland, Scandinavia, Italy and parts of the United States. The minuscule German empire gets bigger every year, and trains alone have become insufficient to fulfil the ambition. To reach places beyond Germany, the founders have also built a busy waterway and a model airport, from which small planes take off on metal poles and disappear through a vinyl curtain, and every now and then there is a pre-planned fire when a plane nose-dives on the runway, and miniature fire engines rush in reliably from the depot. Eventually the Wunderland staff – there are about 320 of them – may build the entire world, with a track running around or through it.

All serious railway modellers will tell you that making a big small model is not just a question of scaling up a small small model. There is the particular problem of supplying the correct voltage for the trains, and another one for power and light elsewhere. Weight becomes a consideration, as does the ventilation system, as does the ability to ensure that a single fault doesn't short-circuit the entire display. And there must be enough variety for the visitor to feel that it's not just one damn mountain pass after another (an early survey found that the railway itself would mostly attract men, but that women would be more attracted by the exacting detail of the landscapes). But the logistical struggles encountered by the team at Miniatur Wunderland somehow come across as both charming and hilarious, no matter how much their narrators wrap them up in high drama and exclamation marks ('The whole system crashed on the eve of the opening when someone turned off the wrong switch!'; 'Trains fell off a bridge and landed on a tiny crowd!'). The difficulties of building small on a big stage are succinctly summed up by Joachim Jürs, Wunderland's head of technical: 'You can't just walk into a store and say, "Give me everything you have, I'm building the largest model railway in the world!"'

But if you did decide to build the largest model railway in the world, one that incorporated both countries and continents, what sort of world would that be?

If you follow the directions from the real train station, and pass the crowds gathering outside the Elbphilharmonie, the sparkling new concert hall designed by Herzog & de Meuron, you will reach the Speicherstadt, which, as you may expect in this region of superlatives, is the largest warehouse district in the world. Some way along there's an unimposing doorway, which leads to drab stone steps, which, three floors up, ushers one into an unimpressive entrance to the miniature railway. The ceilings are low and exposed, the lights are unflattering, the signposting is bad, the gift shop is garish: it is immediately clear that this is a place of engineering and endeavour rather than art or cool. It is an enthusiast's giant attic, albeit one that does go on rather a bit, through several floors and nation states and continents. And it's a big hit. I look at the photos I took of the place, and they show one thing above all others: awed people peering over for a closer look.

Miniatur Wunderland is the vision of Frederik Braun. In July 2000, when he was thirty-two, Braun was in Zurich shopping with friends when he wandered idly into a store selling model railways. At the time he was running a successful Hamburg dance club called Voilà, but after ten years he was getting tired of the nightlife. The model railways in the shop reminded him of the modest layouts of his childhood, and the ambition he shared with his twin brother Gerrit of someday running a large display in the shared basement of their two adjacent houses. It was then, he says, that he suddenly had the idea of building the largest model railway in the world, and he phoned Gerrit back in Hamburg to check online as to how big this would have to be. Gerrit thought he was nuts.

After the fourth phone call, Gerrit was coming round to the idea, as was their business partner, Stephan Hertz. Fairly soon they had won the trust of the banks and local business community, and found their location, a warehouse once used to store coffee. The railway was to be at 'HO' scale (roughly 1:87, with 5/8th of an inch between each rail, the standard size of table railways first popularised in Germany in the 1950s). They calculated they would need €1.5m to launch as a paying exhibit in August 2001, and could break even, with 15 employees, on 300 visitors a day. They rented 1,600 square metres and planned to open when the first 250 square metres was completed. An advert for model makers appeared in the newspapers *Bild* and *Hamburger Abendblatt*.

There were 150 applicants, and the Brauns held auditions involving wood and plaster on the dance floor of their night club. As much emphasis was placed on imagination and humour as on technical experience. Gerhard Dauscher, the model maker employed to lead construction, remembers that he was keen to recruit those whose lives were filled with more than models. 'An open mind for human desires and aspirations, for resting and hunting, love and hate – all of this is essential for a model landscape to mirror real people and real life.' He was also looking for those with a firm appreciation of beauty, believing that 'only in this way is it possible to build a cliff beckoning for a climb, or to create a meadow [where] one would like to rest. Or as I always say, "Only if you can see yourself wherever you look, then you have understood model making!".'

Twenty people were hired, and they worked on Germany first. Initially this wasn't real Germany – an accurate depiction of Hamburg only appeared a year after opening – but a combination of 'Middle Germany' and a fictional place called Knuffingen. Some 200 trains found their way through or around a landscape of mountain ranges, fields of cabbages and sunflowers and cattle, castles, a fairground with a large Ferris wheel, a theatre playing *Romeo and Juliet*, a miniature golf course. Within these there are jokes, tiny details that visitors may believe they are the first to spot: a couple having sex in the sunflowers, a UFO flying over mountains, a Google street-mapping car, the blue portable toilets at a rock concert. In Knuffingen, 1,000 metres of railway track are complemented by the Faller Car System, a computerised road network in which 400 cars are magnetically propelled by rechargeable battery along a thin wire installed under a road. Cars and their tiny drivers skim through the city on their way to the office or the shops; speeding motorists are apprehended by police; every vehicle, apart from those of the emergency services, indicates before turning and obeys traffic lights. A combination of infrared signalling and a computerised induction system ensures the routes are not predetermined, but calculated individually for each car depending on the locations of other cars; traffic jams are thus avoided, unless they are pre-planned. The road network, which is every bit as impressive as the rail network, runs for over a mile, and in the last fifteen years fire engines have raced to 780,000 incidents.

At the end of my visit I couldn't decide whether Miniatur Wunderland was stupefyingly impressive or stupefyingly deranged, but of course it was both. Certainly this miniature world has brought a huge amount of pleasure to millions, and has boosted Hamburg's economy. The place consistently ranks in the top ten permanent tourist attractions in Europe, behind London's British Museum and Madame Tussauds, ahead of the Uffizi and the Pompidou Centre. But I was unnerved by the maniacal expansion, the hundreds of thousands of work hours spent on extending something so seemingly pointless. Had our own world reached its apotheosis, with nothing left to do but digest and duplicate it?

In the many interviews with (and articles by) the Braun twins, they had never offered a grand philosophy of their great model beyond its greatness, or their own ambition and passion. For them, the miniature brings joy and elucidation through careful observation – just *marvel* at the damn thing and get happy – and the philosophers can go hang.

But Miniatur Wunderland is more than a private ambition or pastime now: it has become an industry of its own, a huge commercial reckoning. By 2016, approximately €20m had been spent on expanding the model to 7,000 square metres, and the venture was in handsome profit. More than a million people paid between €10 and €13 for each visit, and the merchandise section – books, models, DVDs – had a long queue at the checkout; there was even a Miniatur Wunderland Monopoly set, with Schloss Neuschwanstein in Bavaria taking the place of Park Lane. In fact, the gift shop revealed that there *was* a simple philosophy to the place: the philosophy of escape. Viewing the world from on high created a sense of limitless possibility. 'Up there, you can be anyone you want to be,' Gerrit Braun has proclaimed, as if auditioning for a Broadway musical. But was 10 miles of optimistic amusement sufficient? In a city such as Hamburg, which has so much history upon its shoulders, was it wrong to hope for something more meaningful?

The railway was always a thing to miniaturise the world. When the earliest intercity lines opened in the 1830s, those who rode upon them believed the usefulness of life would double. Their journeys – initially between Liverpool and Manchester, but very soon afterwards between any locations that wished to join the modern age – were reduced by half or more. Everything moved faster as the world appeared to shrink. But a century later, as more private and seemingly more convenient methods of transport became available, and the network retrenched, the train gradually also adopted another mantle: there was the slow train, the stopping train, the neglected train. Certainly the steam train. And it is this kind of train that model enthusiasts celebrate most keenly – the *idea* of the train, the idealised train. Train layouts tend to portray the state of the world before the state of mind of those portraying it turned nostalgic.

So perhaps the politics at Miniatur Wunderland was in the model itself: only from within could one ascertain what was important to a couple of young Germans rebuilding the world one metre at a time. To most visitors, the trains themselves – about 1,000 of them, with 10,000 wagons – have long since been the support act to the minuscule recreation of the landscapes through which they run (by the autumn of 2016, there were about 260,000 figurines in the model, about 3,500 of which get stolen annually; the loss is elevated by the owners, who refer to their figurines being 'kidnapped'). But what sort of world was being memorial-ised? In 'America', for example, which opened in 2003, Las Vegas took centre stage. More than 30,000 LEDs were installed, and when the house lights dim (which they do every fifteen minutes), it becomes by far the brightest place in the entire model. The founders have explained that they chose to build Vegas, rather than New York or Hollywood, because of the casinos, and the ability to shrink the world twice. Many of the diminished cities in Vegas are also in Hamburg – the Luxor with its pyramid, New York-New York with its Statue of Liberty, Paris with its Eiffel Tower – miniatures of miniatures, half the known world assembled in one corner of a low-ceilinged warehouse on the fringe of the Baltic Sea.

Beyond the expanse of Vegas, the rest of America turns scale on its head. 'The real Grand Canyon is 450 kilometres long and formed in millions of years,' the tour guide in Hamburg explains. 'The Grand Canyon in the Wunderland is not quite as long, and it didn't take millions of years to grow. For the constructors, however, it presented a great challenge . . .' A couple of feet away, Key West gives way to Cape Canaveral, which is just east of Mount Rushmore, which nestles very close to Yosemite. Scattered around there is a SeaWorld show, a functioning oil well, a shoot-out at a train station, giant redwoods and an electric Amtrak gliding through the Everglades – an awfully compressed adventure. One would have to have a steel track through one's heart to complain that the geography was a bit askew – this is entertainment, not school – but still: a 'Wunderland Eurotunnel' connecting Hamburg and the United States?

Italy, which has recently attained its micro-Venice, has so far taken four years to build. There's the Spanish Steps, the Colosseum, a little St Peter's with a little pope, and many cute local characteristics such as deliberately outsize piles of spaghetti and mafiosi up to no good at a building site. Trains have not quite been forgotten (there's a big multi-platform terminus in Rome), but the big draw is undoubtedly Vesuvius, built from resin and real volcanic rock, computerised to erupt at regular intervals and engulf Pompeii below it (one is tempted to proclaim, 'People of Pompeii! Did you learn nothing from what happened just fifteen minutes ago? Run for your lives!'). The designers couldn't decide whether to construct ancient bustling Pompeii on the eve of the big eruption or present-day Pompeii with archaeologists and tourists, so they built both, and they found the two had one thing in common: sandals.

In August 2009, politics entered Wunderland in a direct way. The owners invited six political parties in Germany to design their own utopia, and gave each of them one square metre to display what they considered to be most important for the nation (and presumably their potential voters) in the years to come – a manifesto at 1:87 scale. When *Der Spiegel* came to assess the results a month before the general election, it found each party playing to form, and most with good humour. The jingoistic Christian Social Union transformed Berlin's Unter den Linden into a modern version of Oktoberfest, featuring businessmen in lederhosen working on laptops; the Left Party chose to mount an anti-discrimination rally; the Free Democratic Party showed a gay wedding; the Green Party designed a pastoral scene of solar energy and wind turbines; while Angela Merkel's Christian Democratic Union painted 9,000 small people to represent the German flag. The experiment was repeated in 2013, by which time the parties had begun to parody themselves. The CDU showed a black policeman escorting children and the elderly over a road in the shadow of the European flag; figures representing the Social Democratic Party were building a bridge between the dual encampments of 'education' and 'equal opportunities'; the FDP featured gay parents queuing to donate blood. And in this way did Miniatur Wunderland present its own manifesto, an honourable and slightly queasy fantasy of punctual trains in the best of all fair worlds. The devil in all of us may, against our more noble judgement, wish for a large Terry Gilliam-style foot to descend and crush it all.

Within its parallel reality, the future at MiWuLa looks bright, and shows no sign of accommodating the world's escalating terrors. France is up next, and then a tunnel linking it to Britain, which means the addition of both the Eiffel Tower and Big Ben – the usual pattern of the most notable biggest things consistently inspiring the most notable smallest things. There are plans too for Africa and Asia, and after that there's always Antarctica (with its chilly central train station – who knew!). Ten thousand square metres have now been licensed to cover expansion to 2028, which will take the track length to about 12.5 miles. The attraction the Brauns have created in Hamburg resembles nothing so much as a souvenir brochure for the entire world. Stereotypes abound, intricacies are manifold, complexities are banished: it's a fabulous place if you don't believe it exists and don't take it too seriously. But this puts it at stark odds with the rest of the model railway world, which takes itself very seriously indeed.

When Sir Rod Stewart visited Miniatur Wunderland in September 2013 his trains were already out of the closet. That is, he had confessed his hobby to the world, and it was a confession, he admitted later, that was not always easy. Too often railway modellers were seen as misfits or loners, one signal box short of a layout. In the US, where Stewart has lived since his tax exile in the mid-'70s, they're a little more accepting, he says, with many fans regarding his hobby as one of his more adorable British foibles. Rod Stewart has a hot new model, and she's not even blonde; his favourite tracks are not musical; et cetera, et cetera.

When Stewart – more than 100 million records sold, more than 30 top ten UK singles – spoke to an incredulous Piers Morgan about his love of train modelling on CNN in 2011, it was as if the two men were speaking different languages. When Morgan first mentioned his train set, Stewart responded as if he'd just insulted his wife. 'A train *set?*' Stewart repeated. His layout was 1,500 square feet.

'What does it bring you?' Morgan asked.

'It's like any hobby, man. It's just brilliant. I don't get stressed, but if I do get a little stressed I go, "Fuck it, I'm going upstairs," and spend a couple of hours. I get permission from Penny: "Is it all right if I disappear to the third floor and just work on my hobby?"'

'Is it the size of this room?' Morgan asked him in the ground-floor library of his palatial home in Beverly Hills (Regency furniture, Pre-Raphaelite paintings, Celtic football scarf).

'It's the length of this house!' Rod Stewart said.

'How many trains do you have?'

Stewart turned around to look at the producer. 'Are people

still watching this?' he wondered aloud. 'It's not a question of trains,' he explained patiently. 'It's a question of scale and detail. I base my layout on the 1940s New York Central and Pennsylvania line. I love it, man, I really do, and I take it everywhere with me.' (Stewart often tours with vast cases of trains and track, setting up layouts in hotel suites.)

'Do you like being the driver or the station master?' Morgan continued, as if referring to coded sexual behaviour.

'Now don't take the piss! I don't wear a little hat! It's a lovely hobby – it's like reading a book or painting a picture. It's three-dimensional. You know, it's wonderful.' It was the surest defence of a hobby anyone could mount: it was love pure and simple, Stewart confirmed, and if you didn't get it then the loser was you.

Stewart came out publicly in the December 2007 issue of American *Model Railroader*. The singer had coyly set up the feature himself. 'Having been a model railroader for 20 years,' he wrote to the publisher Terry Thompson, 'and an avid reader of your magazine for longer, I thought you may be interested in publishing some photos of my layout.' The magazine was impressed with his photos, and was bowled over when staff members saw his layout up close.

'Hall of fame rock-n-roller unwinds after a concert by kitbashing and scratchbuilding,' they gleefully explained in a press release, as if they could hardly believe it themselves. His model was 23 feet wide and 124 feet long, and was called the Grand Street & Three Rivers Railroad. Like Miniatur Wunderland, Stewart's railway was at the HO scale of 1:87. It had more than 100 structures, some taller than 5 feet. There were also streets, cars, billboards, people, trees and many trains. During busy periods there would be thirteen engines operating at once. He swore by the Digitrax Digital Command Control. 'I pity a man who doesn't have a hobby like this one – it's just the most supreme relaxation,' Stewart told the magazine's readers, perhaps the only people who didn't need telling.

'I don't wear a little hat!': Rod Stewart enjoys his layout in Beverly Hills.

Before anyone knew it, model railroading had become the new rock 'n' roll. Once Rod was out, they were all out. Roger Daltrey had a nice middle-aged layout in the attic, as did the late Davy Jones of the Monkees. But no one loved a painted gasometer or an uncoupled bogie more than Neil Young.

Young's association with small trains began at the age of four, when his dad laid out a Marx Santa Fe diesel at their home in Ontario, and he thought it was the finest thing ever. A few years later his ambitions broadened, and he learnt that the train to have was not a Marx but a Lionel, the aficionado's favourite. He got his first Lionel loco in his early teens, and constructed his first solo track in the basement. He told *Classic Toy Trains* magazine about frequent floods and occasional electric shocks as his Lionels battled through regardless.

The Lionel Manufacturing Company was founded in 1902. Joshua Lionel Cowen, one of nine children born to Jewish New York immigrants from Eastern Europe, had already tried his hand with other patented inventions – a snazzy new torch, a portable electric fan – when he began to wonder about the small tin-plate trains he had seen running around circular tracks in shop windows. These were probably of German origin, made either by Märklin or its rival Bing. (The German toy industry, which was centred in Nuremberg since the end of the fourteenth century, dominated the early world of model trains – first with clockwork models, and then primitive electric versions; the dominance lasted until the First World War. The first documented model railway, however, was not German but French, laid out, or at least paid for, by Napoleon III for his three-year-old son Prince Imperial. A photograph from 1859 suggests a single clockwork train running over a viaduct on a figure-8 formation in a private park in Saint-Cloud.)

Cowen copied what he could from the Germans, and grasped two opportunities. He marketed his Lionel trains specifically for Christmas; and he improved the system of propulsion – promoting an elaborate way of hooking his trains into the burgeoning urban mains electricity system by means of a transformer: 'What real-live wide-awake boy is not interested in electricity?' he wondered. 'Is there any better way than to have a perfect model as an instructor?' (Electricity for Lionel trains was supplied by a central third rail, a popular system now largely abandoned by other manufacturers.) Cowen also realised that his initial sales could soon be supplemented by additional trains and track and bridges, enabling the construction of 'a wholly equipped miniature road'. And thus was material desire established in the head of young male American society.

The train and starter track was only the first step towards a proper layout, and the proper layout guaranteed lucrative long-term brand loyalty. There were so many gauges and standards to choose from (from the Germans initially, and then from Lionel's earliest American rivals Ives and British competitors such as Hornby and Bassett-Lowke) that it became troublesome or impossible to mix and match. Lionel went further still. 'Wow! It's a Lionel' read a tiny billboard that impressionable minds were encouraged to place trackside – a smart corollary to post-purchase remorse, and perhaps the earliest example of product placement within a product one had already purchased. But how to choose, when presented with the lavish Lionel colour catalogues, between the Texas

Special Two-Unit Diesel with Magne-Traction and horn and headlight and smoke mechanism and the 2035 Sante Fe Diesel, also with Magne-Traction and horn and headlight and smoke mechanism?

Neil Young chose – or was given – the 2035 Santa Fe. He says he ran that train for years before he was able to afford a companion (it was a big, heavy tin-plate machine and it ran on wide rails set almost 3 inches apart). When, years later, he could afford to buy all the Lionel trains he wanted, he went a step further and bought a stake in the company. He continued to develop his control unit, and he invested a lot of hope in a digital device that would recreate accurately the sound of the trains as they sped by. He also developed a modelling persona, writing an online Lionel agony aunt column under the name Clyde Coil. If, for example, you were having classic voltage and throttle dilemmas, and you asked a question such as 'Do I really need 18 volts to run Trainmaster Command Control?', Clyde/Neil would solve those problems with ease. 'Absolutely not! In fact, you can run TMCC at any voltage you like. Running at lower voltages actually increases yer low speed control, while it does decrease yer top speed. The pulses of power still come through yer LCRU to yer loco's motor, but at say 15 volts yer gonna get more fine control at slow speeds. That's a good reason to keep and use an old ZW for yer power source, especially in the YARD!' That was written, apparently, by the same man who wrote 'Heart of Gold' and 'Harvest'.

In his 2012 autobiography *Waging Heavy Peace*, Young did a Rod Stewart and explained his passion to the rest of the world. He may have hesitated before doing so: his earlier experience of reluctantly coming out to his band mates left him wondering whether his obsession was something best left in his barn. David Crosby and Graham Nash had been spending time in his studio. In a break from recording, Young saw Crosby looking at one of his train rooms packed with rolling stock and then giving Nash a glance that said, 'This guy is cuckoo. He's gone nuts. Look at this obsession.' Young said he shrugged it off. He *needs* his sacred hobby, he writes. 'For me it is a road back.'

What so attracts people with such amplified lives to a life of little trains running back and forth? Rock stars are seemingly attracted to the same three things that make many adult males spend upwards of a half billion dollars annually on the pastime. There's the desire to completely control one's chosen environment (Rod Stewart dominating the 1940s landscape of his childhood; the Braun brothers in Hamburg eventually controlling the world). There's the desire to escape the real world for a few hours or days by entering a landscape of one's own creation. And there's the attempt, however futile, to recapture or re-evaluate a childhood.

In his memoir, Neil Young revealed that the trains he was playing with now were partly for himself and partly for his son Ben, who was born quadriplegic. 'Sharing the building of the layout together was one of our happier times.' Young devised a controller with a large red button suitable for Ben's limited mobility, and his ability to see the cause and effect of his actions empowered him. But the effect leaves a therapeutic impression on the father too. Young builds his layouts not with shop-bought bridges and scenery but with material from the natural world – stumps of local redwood and spreads of local moss. In his imagination 'the railroad has fallen on hard times. A drought has ensued. Track work, once accomplished by hardworking teams of Chinese labourers, has been left dormant.' Young explains that the display and layout create a Zen-like experience for him. 'They allow me to sift through the chaos, the songs, the people, and the feelings from my upbringing that still haunt me today. Not in a bad way, but not in an entirely good way either.'

Ron Hollander, the author of a rewarding history of Lionel trains, believes that the company – and by extension, model trains in general – were marketed as an antidote to the vagaries of adult life. 'Whether extolling the grimy locomotive engineer as American hero, or equating a gift of electric trains with fatherly love, Lionel provided beguilingly easy solutions to complex social problems.' Hollander recounts that far from being the perfect father himself, founder Joshua Lionel Cowan would often bully his son or ignore him for prolonged periods. 'Things didn't work out the way Cowan promised they would if we played with his trains,' Hollander writes, 'not for us and not for him.' Modern collectors – the classic baby boomers who missed out on the best Lionel engines in their childhood or now regretted selling their collections – may fare no better. 'Once Lionel offered the promise of a fulfilled childhood. Now it holds the possibility of something better than eternal life – the illusion of starting over.'

Hollander reasons that when grown-ups open the box of a new train it is as if we are opening it for the first time at the age of eight, our souls new and unscathed. A bassinet of sadness inevitably awaits. But there is an alternative and more optimistic interpretation, and in this scenario model railways again perform a role with which we've become familiar from so much of the wider miniature world. As with the doll's house and the model village, they make us re-examine a familiar object with a keener eye, and understand more. For Neil Young to find a reflection of his own demons in narrow steel tracks is telling: model railways are a repository of personal hope, and sometimes redemption. The fact that things do not always proceed in a calm and straightforward fashion – perilous curves, derailments, mockery from the sidelines – may reflect how well model railways approximate real life, which was usually what their makers intended, and often what their owners would do anything to avoid.

The search for the lost ideal: Alec Garrard and his Temple of Jerusalem.

Mini–break, 1992:
Jerusalem's Temples

In August 1992, the German novelist W.G. Sebald recalled a journey he had made around the storied flatlands of East Anglia. As with most of his trips, and true to his melancholic soul, the author found mostly desolation and ghosts. Sebald – or his narrator, the distinction is purposefully unclear – recalls the adventure in his meandering and mesmeric book *The Rings of Saturn*, an account preoccupied with scale and perspective, and by distant and lofty views over the architecture of ruin.

In the book, Sebald's two favourite vantage points are a) the solitary figure in a vast landscape and b) the discerning aerialist gazing down on a small scene below. He also loves a bizarre miniature, and recounts the story of an edible model of the Ottoman siege of Esztergom in 1543, 'created by a confectioner to the Viennese court, which Empress Maria Theresa, so it is said, devoured in one of her recurrent bouts of melancholy'. Eating a model of a battle: has there ever been a sadder example of human omnipotence?

Towards the end of his journey, Sebald comes to a place in Suffolk he names Chestnut Tree Farm, an ancient moated house, where he meets a farmer named Thomas Abrams. Abrams is a modeller, and an obsessive one; by now you may justifiably be wondering if other types of modellers exist. He is building, in a barn, from clay and wood, the Temple of Jerusalem (also known as Herod's Temple, the Second Temple, the Third Temple, the Temple of the Jews, Solomon's Temple or just the Temple). He has been doing this for a reassuringly long time – more than twenty years – and when he wasn't farming he'd be attending to his fully scalable walls and ant-ready anterooms, and thousands of tiny figures, each a little crude in their dress and purpose – but wouldn't you be at three-quarters of an inch high?

One problem for Abrams was that the plans for his model kept on changing in tiny ways. Not a month would go by without some smart Sebag uncovering some new evidence about the precise height of a column or atrium, which would call into question the height of the adjacent antechamber. It was enough to drive Abrams to despair. One visitor, an American evangelist (several of these had come to visit, along with ultra-Orthodox Jews and Jehovah's Witnesses), asked Abrams whether he was inspired by divine intervention. The answer alas was no: 'If it had been divine intervention, I said to him, why would I have had to make alterations as I went along?'

At a scale of 1:100, the model measured approximately 12 feet by 20 feet. Sebald had visited it before, and reports hardly any visible progress from one year to the next. There are, however, new allusions. When Abrams shows him an aerial view of how the Temple site looks today, Sebald notices how much the gleaming Dome of the Rock resembles the new Sizewell B nuclear reactor on Suffolk's coast. And there is some good recent news on the question of his friend's sanity. Thomas Abrams's family and neighbours had, over the years, begun to wonder about his mental health, and whether, in Sebald's brutal terminology, spending his time in an unheated barn, getting deeper and deeper into a fantasy world, 'fiddling about with such an apparently never ending, meaningless and pointless project' to the detriment of applying to the European Union for farm subsidies like his neighbours and all the other farmers in England, wasn't perhaps taking things a bit far. But then one day Lord Rothschild pulled up in a very expensive car and offered to house the completed project in the atrium of his mansion, and people began to regard the whole project, and its maker, with a modicum of respect. Then another visitor turned up at the barn and suggested it would be wonderful if Abrams would think about building a life-size version of his model – i.e. a real Temple of Jerusalem – in the Nevada desert not far from Las Vegas, where it would stand as a beacon of virtue in a state of sinners, and family and friends began to think a little less of the project again.

'My model is thought to be the most accurate replica of the Temple ever produced,' Thomas Abrams concluded, and this was indeed some proclamation, for the endeavour has some remarkable antecedents. For those keen on modelling, rebuilding the Temple has long been the Holy Grail. The

Temple was a monument to the imagination even when it stood, and two millennia later it continues to carry enough historical-religious baggage to incite conflict among nations. 'It has become the most potent symbol of the human search for a lost ideal,' writes the classical historian Simon Goldhill. 'We need a special sort of archaeology for this great building of the world, an archaeology that uncovers not so much rock and dust as the sedimented layers of human fantasy, politics and longing.' Fantasy and longing have always appealed to the miniaturist, as have the rigours of a lifelong challenge and obsessional sleuthing. And through it all, family members may pull their hair out, and death may precede completion.

But at the end of it we will be rewarded with an education. There were in fact three temples. The precise date of the first, the Temple of Solomon, is uncertain, but we can be sure of its destruction by the Babylonians in 587 BCE. By 515 BCE it had been rebuilt by Zerubbabel, and was again desecrated under the command of Antiochus IV in 167 BCE. The third Temple was built by King Herod from 19 BCE, and in CE 70 it was destroyed again – and finally – by the Romans. Most modellers have concentrated their miniature reconstructions on the first and the third examples, although the third is often called the second. Here already was an issue: if the listing of the monuments themselves caused confusion, what hope remained for their accurate reconstruction?

The earliest latter-day models were based on descriptions in the Hebrew bible and Talmud, with additional suggestions from the first-century classical scholar Josephus. The largest and most daring example of Solomon's First Temple was constructed in wood in 1628 by the Dutch rabbi Jacob Judah Leon, the proportions comparable to the model in Thomas Abrams's Suffolk barn. The work made such an impression when shown in Amsterdam that its creator was recommended by letter to Sir Christopher Wren; by the time the model appeared in London, to be swiftly adopted by the early Freemasons as inspiration for their first lodges, he had already become known as Judah Leon Templo.

A man named Gerhard Schott constructed a larger wooden model in 1692, initially for use in an opera in Hamburg (it may still be seen in the city's Stiftung Historische museum though not, alas, in Miniatur Wunderland). Measuring 13 feet tall by 80 feet round, this too was shipped over to an eager crowd in London, where it was seen at the Opera House in the Haymarket by King George I and probably Sir Isaac Newton (who wrote a lengthy illustrated treatise on it). The model was advertised as rich in gold, silver and jewels, with 6,700 pillars and 1,500 chambers: 'The complete masterpiece . . . has not its like in the universe.' But it did have a lot of competition. The theologian and mathematician William Whiston held regular lectures at Button's Coffee House in Covent Garden, and in 1730 announced that he had built a model of the Temple to rival Schott's. One critic who saw both was incensed: how was it possible that two modellers couldn't agree upon a single thing?

The largest model of all, a rugged ochre imagining of Jerusalem at the time of Herod's Temple almost 2,000 years ago, was the size of a model village. Built in the mid-1960s by the archaeologist Michael Avi-Yonah at 1:50 scale, it was constructed with materials as close as possible to those in use at the time of King Herod: stone, marble, wood, iron and copper. It now occupies approximately 1,000 square metres of the Israel Museum, to the west of the Old City it depicts, but it was previously in the grounds of the Holy Land Hotel in another part of town, and to transport it in 2006 required sawing it into 100 sections. A brochure provides a fulsome guide to its painstaking detail: 'On the northern side was the Place of Slaughtering, with marble tables, posts and hooks . . . Continuing along the wall, you pass the Ophel Quarter. The Ophel Quarter was so high, according to the Talmud, that from its top "an Arab with a spear looked like a flax worm".' Scale within scale. Visitors are not allowed to walk over or within the model, only around it, the walls coming up to their knees.

Biblical-sounding as it was, Thomas Abrams was not his real name. Sebald had invented it to protect his friend, and to distance himself from straight reportage. His real name was Alec Garrard, and in addition to being a farmer and modeller he was also a Methodist lay preacher and wildlife painter. He did indeed live and build in Suffolk, and his model in his barn on his fifty-acre Moat Farm in Fressingfield was almost finished when he died, after thirty years' work, in 2010 at the age of eighty. Perhaps, like the French family 'putting the finishing touches' to the Eiffel Tower in their living room, almost finishing was always the best place to be. Even if Garrard had outlived Methuselah he might not have welcomed completion. Finishing a large model invites not only judgement but the surrender of control – two concessions rarely beneficial in any walk of life. In the miniature world, completion also ushers in a terrible void, and the admittance once again of unwelcome realities.

When he posed for pictures at the side of his Jerusalem, Alec Garrard fitted the bill: slightly owlish, uneasy in media situations, always a tie beneath the jumper. He began modelling planes and ships as a teenager, and when his interests turned to religion he built a 27-inch by 55-inch replica of the Jerusalem Tabernacle. When it was time to build his huge model of Herod's Temple, which relied for its accuracy on the codified descriptions in the oral Jewish divinity known as the Mishnah, he hoped it would serve as an educational tool for students and scholars, and would provide some evidence, if it were needed, of the value of perseverance and application. He had conquered – or almost conquered – an Everest of myth and historical longing, and, with 100,000 tiny clay bricks, had produced a monumental piece of personal worship.

At the last count, Garrard's model included about 4,000 clay figures, all hand-baked and hand-painted, and some additionally adorned with tissue paper. Each were tasked with a specific role. Some were praying, some bartering, some slaughtering, some washing, others debating, and others lighting oil lamps. Many were just wandering about the steps and cavernous halls, a chorus emphasising scale. There were also sixteen scenes with tiny dolls depicting the life of Jesus, with their creator gleefully claiming that 'no one has ever been able to find all of them'. The figures were representational, and as such took their place in a grand procession of symbolic dolls dating back to Egyptian shabtis. But the secrecy of their location was more than just a parlour game: it spoke of the possessive nature of a pursuit so particular and exacting that only one person – its creator – could possibly have all the answers. Playing God in the Kingdom of Jerusalem: miniaturists don't usually pursue that sort of purple aggrandisement, but perhaps they won't refuse it if it comes their way.

A goddess of small things: Zaha Hadid in her London office.

Chapter Seven

The Future Was a Beautiful Place

A Vision
by Simon Armitage

The future was a beautiful place, once.
Remember the full-blown balsa-wood town
on public display in the Civic Hall?
The ring-bound sketches, artists' impressions,

blueprints of smoked glass and tubular steel,
board-game suburbs, modes of transportation
like fairground rides or executive toys.
Cities like *dreams*, cantilevered by light.

And people like us at the bottle bank
next to the cycle path, or dog-walking
over tended strips of fuzzy-felt grass,
or model drivers, motoring home in

electric cars. Or after the late show –
strolling the boulevard. They were the plans,

all underwritten in the neat left-hand
of architects – a true, legible script.

I pulled that future out of the north wind
at the landfill site, stamped with today's date,
riding the air with other such futures,
all unlived in and now fully extinct.

(From *Tyrannosaurus Rex Versus
the Corduroy Kid*, 2006)

Keen to build your own Italian villa? You will need three knives, for a start. The first needs to be long on the blade and straight on the cutting edge. The second requires a pointed tip intended for a building's ornaments. And number three must have a rounded edge for circular work and curves of every description. You will also need a steel T-square and a press capable of gluing and flattening, a cutting board made from beech or pear tree, and finally a cream-coloured sheet of 'crayon paper' – firm but not hard in texture, not so spongy that it absorbs too much paste, and easily tinted to make it look like brickwork.

This list comes from *The Art of Architectural Modelling in Paper* (1859) by T.A. Richardson, a book that broke new ground. While running his own successful architect's practice in Cheshire, Richardson had noticed how many of his students needed particular instruction on the one thing he claimed would make the difference between success and failure in their lives: model making. He claimed that the skill could be mastered by anyone with patience and the right tools. He provided many tips and notes, including advice on the desired strength and firmness of a wall or roof: 'One thickness, two thicknesses, three thicknesses, and so forth.'

The process of actually constructing your mini villa ('The student must carefully draw each elevation of the building the full height, from the ground line to the top of the blocking') goes on for fifty pages, and although Richardson doesn't guarantee that building the model will make you an architect, the application required to master the complexity of his advice does guarantee that you don't become an architect if you aren't truly sure you want to be one.

To his credit, Richardson also acknowledged that a model may create as many problems as it solves, and this was the case with the most famous classical architectural miniature of all – the Great Model of St Paul's Cathedral by Sir Christopher Wren. Made from oak, lime wood and plaster, painted in colours of stone and lead with gilded details, it cost about £600. Yes, that was just the model: in the seventeenth century you could buy a full size palace in Kensington for that. It took more than 2,000 hours to make, and was ready for judgement by August 1674, twenty-three years before the church held its first service. The scale is 1:25, and at 4 metres high by 6 metres long it is monumental (if not quite the dimensions originally suggested by

Charles II, who wanted a model he could wander around in; he settled for examining it from the inside at chest height, with the dome over his head and fragments of light illuminating the sides of the transept). The Great Model, a title which distinguishes it from an earlier attempt, and which is still viewable today in the place it depicts, was made not by Wren but by his joiner William Cleere, while the dome was made by the king's own master plasterer John Grove, and the columns and ornaments – cherubim, statues, garlands – by Cleere's brother Richard. The level of detail was precisely what the royal warrant specified in its demands ('a perpetual and unchangeable rule and direction for the conduct of the whole work'), and Wren regarded it as a beautifully detailed and impressive realisation of his finest creation.

Apparently Wren wept when the model was rejected. There is no official record of why his proposals were not approved by the Rebuilding Commission (composed of civic officials and clergymen), but it is clear that he was undone by the familiar wrecking ball of politics and religion. The scheme may have been judged too elaborate, too modern-European, and too Catholic. The scale and detail of the model may have worked against him; he had left so little to the imagination. Certainly the final version of St Paul's that we know differs substantially from the model: the dome is no longer supported by pillars, there is a secondary cupola, and the dramatic 'Greek Cross' layout has been replaced by a more symmetrical and ornate design.

According to an eighteenth-century family memoir, Wren resolved that henceforth he would 'make no more models . . . which, as he had found by Experience, did but loose time, and subjected his Business many Times, to incompetent judges'. So new plans were submitted primarily on paper, and the final building constantly evolved during its long construction; he did commission a few more models of certain aspects of the cathedral, but he realised the value of keeping things adaptable and fluid. The unsteady balance between the rigidity of a model and the flight of the imagination would continue to challenge architects for the next 300 years.

In the autumn of 2006, I visited the architect Zaha Hadid at her office in Clerkenwell, London. Despite her immense fame and reputation, and despite a list of stunning buildings and prizes to her name, she had yet to build a building in Britain, her home for the last twenty-six years. 'It's ridiculous,' she told me. 'I have no idea why they don't choose me! I can't speculate any more. Nobody has actually come up to me and said, "They don't want you here . . .".'

The anomaly was about to be rectified. She had designed a beautiful small building adjacent to the Victoria Hospital in Kirkcaldy, Fife, an informal drop-in space for cancer patients. It was inspired by a friend of Hadid's named Maggie Keswick Jencks, and the concept was simple: to build a unit away from the immediate clinical concerns of a hospital where a patient may have their spirits raised. Ideally the building would have an expansive view, and an area to contemplate and chat about the latest care choices. Shortly before she herself succumbed to cancer in 1995, Jencks hoped it would be a place where the joy of life would overcome the fear of death, and where, in a word seldom heard in modernist architectural circles, people may feel 'hugged' by a building.

In her office, Zaha Hadid had her own simple description: she was making 'a place where people can chill out'. Other leading architects had also constructed their own Maggie's Centres – Frank Gehry in Dundee, Richard Rogers in London, Foster and Partners in Manchester – but Hadid's commission appeared to throw up particularly complex challenges, not least its proximity to the hospital car park.

She solved the problem by locating her building on the wilderness dipping into a hollow by the edge of the site, facing away from the hospital in an act of defiance. The outside is clad in a black liquid-applied polyurethane. The seamless fold of its steel structure suggested a single cell before it started to multiply. Inside, within the clear and translucent glass walls, the scene is white, the curves and ramps contrasting with the taut external frame and the dynamic overhanging roof. Once again, symbolism: the harsh reality softened by clean comfort and impregnability. 'I think that fundamentally architecture is really about well-being,' Hadid told me. 'Every building you make, people should feel good in it.'

It is, of course, tricky to portray these ideals in a model.

I got the sense that even at the very beginning of her career Hadid had realised there would always be a chasm between what she could explain in foam and chipboard and what she would build in real life. It explains why, more than was the case with most architects, her miniature representations were often abstract art: angular synaptical explosions that had caused the critics to scramble around for new descriptors. Were her structures constructivist, deconstructivist, or post-structualist? And because she was an iconoclast, and a woman too, her supporters (and Hadid herself) questioned whether she would ever be trusted by the patriarchy. At the Royal Academy Summer Show, where Zaha Hadid Architects was a regular exhibitor, her work gradually migrated from the architectural room to the flightier and more splashier work of the main rooms. In her early days she came to acknowledge, with more than a touch of dismay, that her work may as well be art: so little of it ever got near to a hard hat or crane. And very early on she emphasised the value of models to a career that may be judged so uncompromising that the models remained the prime legacy.

After years of drawing and modelling and envisioning on a small scale, her buildings, when they finally appeared, couldn't help but burst with vivid kinetic energy – the creature free of her chains. And they couldn't help but boast weighty girders of philosophy: so much theorising and focused seeing at an intimate and intricate level would finally spread its layers of learning at full dramatic scale in the real world.

* * *

Hadid was born in Iraq, but she established her name at the Architectural Association in London. She had a fearsome reputation, of the sort that genius mavericks love to project, and on my visit she combined an air of imperiousness with the attributes of a comely matron. Her character and physics were both larger than life, a scale that would befit any architect, and when she picked up a model to explain a point – a tall tower yet to be completed – it sat upon her palm like a twig on a sand dune.

Her building in Fife was only a few weeks from its opening, but she took me back to her drawing board to recall its conception. Her earliest paper sketches were free-form action paintings, only later becoming precise renderings. Her models, roughly made from cardboard and Perspex, came a little closer to capturing the vigorous spirit of the proposed building; but even these were impressionistic, one of them no more than a layered cascade of card emphasising its position over a fertile hollow, and another emphasising the flow of natural light. The models were classic matte white, whereas the building was coated with a silicon carbide grit that made it glisten in the sun. Scale was established by a couple of detached human figures on the periphery, also spray-painted white, and a few people exercising inside.

'The idea was that it should be hovering over the edge,' Hadid said, pointing to an acute angle in the card. 'It's like a fold, like one whole piece that just wraps around. These shapes here [she points to triangular cut-outs that resemble birds alighting on the roof] are openings for light . . . inside there are curved walls . . . here you can have a consultation with a nurse, and here you can have a relaxation course, and here is the toilet, and this is the library area, and here is the main kitchen area with this big table where you can have tea and just chat to whoever else is there.'

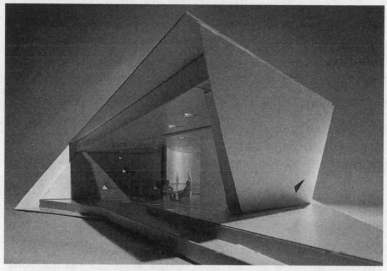

Hovering over the edge: Maggie's Centre takes shape and form.

Even with its sharply angled cantilevered roof, the building was far from the avant-garde anti-gravitational creations that sealed her reputation. In fact, her Fife triumph is often ignored during her career retrospectives, deemed a minor work against her later large-scale achievements. Her first British building was as close to making an entire small house as she would ever get, with a functioning kitchen at the heart of it and a modern domestic decor; in therapy speak, the building 'held' its occupants.

Hadid and her colleagues used the models and photos of the models to explain her plan to her clients and those who would fund it, as well as the contractors who would actually build it. And she used them to explain her ideas to visiting writers more used to verbal expression. I found it impossible to imagine how the Maggie's Centre building would have been realised without first being shown on this tiny scale, but not difficult to imagine how compromising it must have been to reduce a grand vision in this way. Accordingly, in some of her other work in the studio, card and board had been employed purely as work aids, seldom to be seen by anyone but her colleagues. One memorable piece, an impression of the Illinois Institute of Technology Center in Chicago made in 1998, was constructed from a huge stack of card sheets, most of them piled high on the same parallel, a few edged out towards the viewer into vertical columns in the shape of rectangles or pyramids, like a badly shuffled giant poker deck. An observation in *Architectural Record* from 1914 still seemed apt: precisely detailed models 'do not make imagination necessary, and for the same reason they are not works of art'.

The substance of the architectural model has changed over the centuries. The Renaissance favoured mahogany. The nineteenth century brought plaster to the task, while today we model in refined plastics. One sees a philosophical transformation too, dating from the 1960s – a move away from realism to something more abstract and suggestive. But in any material from any age, the model speaks a universal language. We like things we can hold up for examination, things we can peer through and around. We get satisfaction from visualising a whole vast project in one glance, and in different lighting conditions. We appreciate the miniature beginnings of things, and we enjoy the notion that, before architects get to play God, we too – the interested onlooker at an exhibition or open day – may also be the god of small things.

In her encyclopaedic book *Modeling Messages*, the critic Karen Moon quotes the leading contemporary Norwegian American architect Peter Pran: 'Everybody can understand a model; that's the beauty of it. Freehand renderings and three-dimensional computer renderings have great appeal, but models speak to us all.' Above everything, the model represents the *idea* of architecture rather than the reality, even though it may be no more buildable at full scale than constructing a full-size model railway. It puts the world at play.

Over the years, as Zaha Hadid's reputation grew, many of her rough and singular miniatures became precious and prized, for they were unique glimpses into a fiery mind. Often they were the only physical proof that Hadid's vision for so many new creations ever existed. There was the Dutch parliament extension in The Hague (1978, not realised); the Irish prime minister's residence in Dublin (1979, not realised); a redesign of the Grand Building around Trafalgar Square (1985, not realised); and a new scheme for Hamburg's docks (1986, not realised). The future was a beautiful place once.

When the San Francisco Museum of Modern Art mounted a mid-career retrospective of Zaha Hadid's work in 1997, it didn't show photos of her projects, but long, scroll-like paintings. One of the introductory texts explained that she 'designs buildings that look like they explode', which made them sound unsafe even to examine on paper. Of course, by the time I called on her in 2006, a decade before she died at the age of sixty-five, Hadid was a 'paper architect' no more. With the completion of the BMW Plant building in Leipzig and the Phaeno Science Centre in Wolfsburg she had enjoyed both acclaim and recognition, and had created much noise. She was still largely known for her 'spiky' phase, the phase where her buildings looked like the futuristic modular sort drawn by a child with a new geometry set. She had not yet built the structures emblematic of her 'swooning flow' phase, best exemplified by the huge seductive curves at her Olympic Aquatics Centre and the Serpentine Sackler Gallery in London and her Wangjing skyscrapers in China. These later, grander schemes seemed impossible to model, let alone build. But when they did somehow emerge in miniature, after initial imaging on computers, paper and card were deemed insufficient to realise even a half-useful impressionistic version. They were largely made (by external specialist companies) in modern materials, often polyester, wire, metal sheets and – a particular Hadid favourite – clear or sandblasted acrylic. In time, as a few of these models became extraordinary full-size concoctions in the real world, the real world could finally claim to have caught up with the architect's imagination.

Shrinking the world to something Vegas-size: Paris on the Strip shortly after it opened in 1999.

Mini-break, 1998:
Las Vegas Welcomes the World

At the end of the last century, at the apex of his power, the billionaire hotelier Steve Wynn asked me an intriguing question. 'If we could build a hotel that, regardless of the century, was clearly, unequivocally, overwhelmingly the most lovely, elegant, beautiful hotel ever built in the history of the planet, a place where even the people in Johannesburg or Singapore would say, "It's a wonderment", well, wouldn't that be something?'

It would indeed. In its place Steve Wynn built the Bellagio, a condensed version of an Italian village he once visited on holiday. The Bellagio was intended as the latest step in the journey that transformed Las Vegas from sleazeville to convention hub to family vacation spot to luxury resort. The buzzword at the Bellagio was elegance, and it began with the famous dancing fountains out front that rose and fell to Mozart and Vivaldi. It ended somewhere unique for this desert city: with a proper art gallery showing Impressionist masterpieces valued at $300 million. Everything at the Bellagio was a little more expensive, a little swisher, a swirl more opulent than its garish rivals, and, in modelling itself on a tiny promontory on Lake Como that was first inhabited around 400 BCE, it offered the patina of European culture. (It wasn't too fussy about which bits of the culture it adopted either: its Spanish/French signature restaurants Picasso and Le Cirque had no difficulty slipping the hotel's Italian moorings, like Columbus setting off for *spaghetti alle vongole* and damned if he didn't find nouvelle cuisine).

Las Vegas is the place where the world conveniently shrinks from something that is world-size to something that is Vegas size. At some point in the 1980s, developers realised that hotels could do well by offering more than gambling and cheap rooms; they could also offer the myth that a visitor, away from the tables, was partaking of an escapist adventure. So mini-resorts sprung up dressed as the swashbuckling high seas (Treasure Island), Ancient Egypt (the Luxor, shaped like a pyramid), Arthurian legend (Excalibur, with its turrets and jousting tournaments) and the entire rainforest (Mandalay Bay, with its voluminous birds of paradise and, unusually for an Amazonian enterprise, a zinc-deco vodka bar fronted by a statue of Lenin).

All these fantasies hit the jackpot, and it was only a matter of time before developers attracted money for hotels themed upon entire cities. Investors believed that visitors – particularly American visitors – would feel safer in a new environment if they didn't require a passport to get there. So in 1997 modern-day Manhattan appeared on the Strip in the form of New York-New York, a hotel with a Coney Island-style rollercoaster that ran through the hotel lobby, and a replica

Statue of Liberty that was so convincing that it fooled the US Postal Service into using a photograph of it on a postage stamp instead of the original. The Venetian appeared two years later. This boasted the Doge's Palace, canals with gondola rides, a small St Mark's Square ('The finest drawing room in Europe,' Napoleon apparently called it; this was more like a kitchenette), and in every hotel restaurant there were *maître d*'s from Nevada who spoke-a like-a zees. A few months later, Paris opened. This hotel came complete (of course) with a half-size Eiffel Tower, the legs of which straddled the interior of the casino, and a dramatically reduced Arc de Triomphe, at which you could celebrate Napoleonic valour with a crêpe Suzette. What's in play when the desire for replication in miniature extends to entire cities? Hubris, at the very least. A shrinking of curiosity too, and the triumph of pastiche.

How to explain this miniature world in the desert? The more one speaks to those who have adopted Vegas as their home, the more one hears talk of Europe as the phantom and Vegas as the real deal. Local television channels treated the opening of the Bellagio as the high watermark of elegance. On one station, a presenter remarked: 'It's certainly a lot easier to get to than Italy.' To which his colleague replied, 'Not tonight. Tonight, the traffic on the Strip will be real bad.'

Most people still came to Las Vegas for the gambling of course (or 'gaming' as the marketeers insist on calling it, transmuting venality into notions of tactics and sport). At the last count in 2016, *Forbes* valued Steve Wynn's net worth at $2.7 billion, and almost all of this had come from casino hotels. He arrived in Vegas in the 1960s, invested in old-school hotels that have since been demolished, sometimes with Wynn himself pushing the crowd-pleasing button that blew them up, and flourished at the helm of the Golden Nugget, Treasure Island and the Mirage. The Mirage is a hotel on a Polynesian theme, with a small volcano that erupts twice every evening and three times on weekends. (*Of course* it's mindless, but try *not* waiting on the sidewalk to see it.)

'I know what people are like out there in London and Paris and Hong Kong,' Wynn told me in November 1998 as his fountains danced to Handel (water has always been the elemental symbol of power in Vegas). 'They want the same things that people in Syracuse want. They want to go on vacation, be in a fanciful environment and eat in great restaurants. British or Chinese, the leisure conversation is remarkably homogenous. Everybody in China is saying: "Shall we go to London, shall we go to Paris?".' Wynn explained that people wanted sophistication these days, and it had been his desire to build something that satisfied not only their basest instinct but also their soul.

At the Bellagio, what was good for the soul was art. Not long ago, the closest the city had got to art was the Liberace Museum, but now there was real art from the Impressionist salons of Paris. Wynn put up a billboard the Strip had never seen before: 'Coming soon,' it said, 'Van Gogh, Monet, Renoir and Cézanne. With special guests Picasso and Matisse'. The sign soon became known as 'Show me the Monet'.

The notion began in another period of art entirely. Wynn thought, 'Wouldn't it be fabulous to have a Caravaggio behind the front desk?' He imagined it as 'a wonderful statement for the lobby – it would be a greeting experience. And imagine having a Tintoretto or a Titian in the ceiling.' But he soon found he had a problem. 'I'd taken art history at school – several courses, I loved it. But I didn't realise the extent to which the old masters market was dominated by religious subject matter rather inappropriate to Las Vegas. I would have gotten myself and my company in big trouble.' Then Wynn discovered that his favourite period was really Impressionism. 'What's not to like about Renoir?' he asked me. 'It's easy. It's like a training bra. It's like your first three-wheeled bike.' And so, with the aid of a highly respected New York dealer called William Acquavella, Wynn spent two and a half years scouring auction houses and private collections in search of pictures to fill what had become the Bellagio Gallery of Fine Art: two small, velvet-lined rooms and a gift shop just a few steps from the racket of the casino.

Wynn took me on a tour of his acquisitions. His gallery, and his upmarket Picasso restaurant in the basement, contained some remarkable pictures, and several, in the words of the late art critic Robert Hughes, 'that any museum would envy'. Hughes also remarked that the whole Bellagio experience is so bizarre that it's almost enough to make you want to spend a weekend there.

'This is the greatest single female picture that Van Gogh painted in his life,' Wynn told me, standing in front of *Peasant Woman Against a Background of Wheat*. 'It was painted the last week of June of 1890 in a wheat field behind a hotel. This is the equivalent of a *Mona Lisa*-calibre picture.' The painting cost $47.5 million, and Wynn liked the idea that gigantic people from the Midwest could enjoy it for an admission fee of just $10. Wynn saw himself shrinking the world – bringing the art to the people so that the people wouldn't have to go anywhere else.

Since our meeting, the Bellagio collection had been broken up – some pictures sold, some retained by Wynn to display in his restaurants and in his subsequent new hotel, which is called Wynn (or Wynn Las Vegas Resort and Country Club). The Wynn hotel, which looks as if it is plated in gold, is not a resort modelled on a city or culture – or rather it is, but the city and culture is Las Vegas. The other hotels to have opened in the last few years have also gone back to glossy Vegas basics, albeit with less tawdriness and more glamour than their predecessors: the Cosmopolitan, the Linq, Vdara, Aria, Delano. And Wynn himself has also suffered a reversal: at the beginning of 2018 he was accused of sexual misconduct by several former employees, and he subsequently resigned as CEO of Wynn Resorts.

The trend now is all-suite and Trump-vulgar. Many of the new hotels boast of Prada and Hermès boutiques and Ferrari dealerships; some don't even have casinos. The attempt to shrink the rest of the world into a neon nightmare in the

Mojave Desert has hit a speed bump; while the Bellagio, the Paris and the Venetian continue to thrive, there are no plans for similarly themed joints – no plans, for instance, for a miniature London replete with Dickensian pickpockets, Mary Poppins cockneys and a little Big Ben. The old country had once again become too old to bother with.

Why the moratorium? Maybe other European capitals, with their intractable migrant crises and terrorism, and the fearful linking of the two, have rendered themselves too frightening. Or maybe, when people do finally drag themselves away from the all-day buffet, they actually want to see the world shown actual size. But some habits die hard. At its opening, the marketing blurb for the Wynn hotel proclaimed, 'It took Michelangelo four years to complete the ceiling of the Sistine Chapel. Your room took five.'

Still afloat: Philip Warren with his warships in 1956 and 2017.

Chapter Eight

The Perfect Hobby

On Saturday, 20 May 2017, a terrible thing happened to the fleet of the British navy. The US marines and Soviet shipping didn't come out of it well either, and nor did floating arsenals from Germany, France, Italy and Spain. For this was the day, at zero nine hundred hours, that Philip Warren, known to his friends as Phil, a retired stationery supplies impresario from Blandford in Dorset, decided, at the age of eighty-six, for reasons operational, to display his magnificent formation of matchstick battleships for the very last time. Or so the local newspapers had us believe.

The Blandford Forum Corn Exchange, home since the eighteenth century to all manner of agricultural jiggery-pokery, and more recently to the mayor's dinner-dance and bric-a-brac sales, was, for a full weekend, colonised by trestle tables covered in blue baize.

The fleet line-up was impressive, and, to the newly initiated, ridiculous. Mr Warren had made 476 ships, and almost half were on display in Blandford. There were warships of various sizes and functions and nationalities, one of every class put to service by the world's navies since 1945. The

Royal Navy dominated, but the US was strongly represented with four supercarriers and a series of cruisers with aircraft on deck. There were matchstick gun turrets, launchers and anchor chains, and missiles both conventional and nuclear. Almost all of them were painted battleship grey: HMS *King George V*, HMS *Bicester*, USS *New Jersey*, USS *Forrestal*, HMS *Tracker*, HMS *Iron Duke*, and, almost inevitably, the M-class destroyer HMS *Matchless*. The names alone brought tearful recognition from stooping visitors. Philip Warren's matchstick battleships all had a flat bottom, so one could narrow one's eyes and believe they were drifting in still waters. The table with the ships stood next to Blandford Model Railway Club's diorama of the Battle of the Somme.

Mr Warren, white thatched eyebrows over keen eyes, was there too, running through the stories and stats. The big models can take a year to build, the smaller ones a few months. He needed 1,500 matches for a small ship, 5,000 for a large one; he had used approximately 700,000 matchsticks in the course of his modelling career.

He has been building this combustible armada his entire adult life; he was seventeen when he launched HMS *Scorpion* in 1948. His first models were rudimentary, but he learnt as he went along, welcoming advice from senior matchstick men, learning how to bend and glue tiny wood (both matchsticks and the sides of the boxes they came in) to his command. He has never wavered from the 1:300 scale of his first launch, and so a 3-foot modern aircraft carrier, loaded with F-14 Tomcats, dwarfs his early corvettes and frigates. Delightfully, the wings of the F-14s bend back, while the blades on the helicopters revolve. 'What you really need is patience,' he says. This is such an obvious thing, but he takes the time to say it again. 'If you rush, you will fail. Lots of patience. And you can't have a temper or get angry, or the ships will suffer.'

Mr Warren said his hobby is not in the least unusual, or wasn't when he started. 'Every other boy back then' was building models of something, he told me on the telephone a few weeks later. 'Of course, matches were very, very, very common. Everybody used them all the time.' Warren used to build flying aircraft, gliders with a rubber band motor. 'Then I had this yen to build a warship. Lying around was a matchbox that had got wet, and I realized what a lovely thin piece of wood it was. I thought that if I built one model it would get the yen out of my system but it didn't turn out that way, because here we are.'

What makes Mr Warren's fleet unusual is its magnitude and scope, small and huge by turns, like so many professional miniature endeavours. 'Quite unwittingly,' he said, 'I've actually built the history of warships.'

Mr Warren had told his story a few times before. 'One interesting incident was that my father was the steward at the British Legion Club, and we lived on the premises, and as a schoolboy one of my jobs was to clear up after socials and whist drives, and every table had a pile of used matches and one or two used matchboxes on it. I had a ready supply, and then as soon as people started to know about my hobby they started collecting matches for me. I would never run short.'

Warren has never been a smoker, and he has never needed to buy a box of matches himself. 'As I said, people in my home town always saved matches and boxes for me, and I'd soak the boxes in disinfectant water and then the paper all peels off and I dry the wood in metal presses. And one day I suddenly realized that half the boxes they'd given me were actually cardboard and not wood. Panic set in then of course. "This is the end of my hobby!" This was in the '80s, but luckily I was able to keep going, because there was another hobby in those days where people collected matchbox labels, and I came across a chap who came in one day when I was exhibiting and he said he had 60,000 different matchbox labels in his collection, he was the secretary of a society of collectors, and he circulated to all his members, and he came up with a couple of bin bags full of wooden boxes for me. One guy rang me up and he'd been clearing out the house of an uncle who'd sadly passed away, and he opened up this great big cardboard box in his uncle's garden and it was absolutely crammed full of old wooden matchboxes. He actually said to me, "If I hadn't heard you on the radio this morning I'd have put them on the bonfire!"'

Mr Warren had a sign at his shows that explained the various stages of warship construction. 'Matchsticks, matchboxes, nothing else is used.' When pressed, he will say that this is not quite true, as there is also a need for tweezers, sandpaper, Humbrol cement, a ruler, a razor and a hatpin (to make holes). Matches do not come in universal sizes – over the years Mr Warren has noted shrinkage – but he is not too particular about what make of match he uses; even the type sold in large plastic bags from modelling shops (i.e. just wood, with no sulphurous ends) are usable. One modest drawback: 'There's an awful lot of equalizing with sandpaper I have to do.'

Equalising, the process by which a matchsticker ensures each match matches, was also an issue for a man named Donald McNarry. At the time of his death in 2010, Mr McNarry was considered by his peers to be one of the most experienced and accomplished model makers in the world, and he would surely have been satisfied with an obituary in the *Daily Telegraph* that noted how his decking was 'always planked to scale'.

His scale ranged from a size he called 'reasonably miniature' (1:16), right down to 'more miniature' (1:100), but he had a comparable skill as a literary chronicler and populariser. He was the modeller's greatest friend, the man to turn to when your glue wasn't thin enough or you were just unsure what to model next. Other writers on the craft focused on specifics: *The Art of Rigging*, say, or *Planking Techniques for Model Shipbuilders* (with the blurb on the jacket noting: 'Planking is one of the most important, and least often addressed, aspects of ship modelling – until now'). But McNarry concentrated on more general guidance. His bestselling *Ship Models in Miniature* (1975) offered sound advice to those considering taking up the craft semi-professionally, with additional tips on how to discuss your hobby with the taxman. (Was model shipbuilding pleasure, trade or both? When did a model leap from being a toy to becoming an exhibition-standard educational tool?) McNarry also wondered whether, when making ships for someone else, it would be fairer to charge per hour or per ship.

Mr McNarry liked a matchstick when occasion arose, but he also employed balsa wood and firewood, as well as ivory, copper, wire and cotton (for the sails). He made warships when clients requested them, but almost every other ship too: the Portuguese caravel (c.1500), the Dutch *pinasschip* (c.1652), the colonial American sloop (1742), and the screw steamer *Archimedes* (1838). He was most proud of his six-gun royal yacht HMY *Kitchen* (1670), the US clipper *Staghound* (1850), and the four-masted barque *Herzogin Cecilie* (1902).

His ships were made as 'waterline' models (flat bottomed, like Mr Warren's), which he would then place in a diorama of choppy ocean and darkening sky. But he would also make 'full hull', which would usually be displayed on a plinth. Mr McNarry was also a model restorer, the man to call when a museum required help with an eighteenth-century East Indiaman or a nineteenth-century paddle steamer. His own models are to be found in the Smithsonian and the Naval Academy Museum at Annapolis. He said he particularly enjoyed working on the 'crude but sincere' models made by soldiers in the Napoleonic Wars.

Mr McNarry's wisdom ranged from the practical to the

philosophical, and may, with some forbearance, be applied to most pursuits of miniaturisation. 'The trick is, of course, to maintain the maximum hours unvaryingly, week after week, year after year,' he wrote. 'This is not too difficult, the work is absorbing, the self-discipline required eases with application, and the world outside becomes increasingly unpleasant.' I was reminded of something Somerset Maugham observed about another quiet pursuit: 'To acquire the habit of reading is to create for yourself a refuge from almost all the miseries of life.' Miniaturisation as a pastime is ballast: whatever else happens, a hobby is the one thing of which hobbyists can be certain.

McNarry believed that people desired his ships because ships are beautiful things, and because delicate and complicated objects are always appreciated. He found that the more delicate and complicated they are, the more people liked them. But why model at all? Writing with refreshing candour, Mr McNarry did not see many positives. The ships he made rarely satisfied him. He wrote of maintaining 'a meagre lifestyle' with little financial reward. The reality too often dawned: 'Ship models are useless things and their only virtue lies in the accuracy and realism with which they depict the prototype in such a way as to give lasting pleasure to the beholder.'

By profession he was a certified accountant, and it was only upon his retirement that he was able to elevate his modelling from the level of part-time amateur hobby to full-time professional madness. He divided his twilight years into a strict regime (he modelled from 8 a.m.–1 p.m. and

2.30 p.m.–7.30 p.m., seven days a week, fifty-two weeks a year).
He kept his lunches light. His wife Iris predeceased him.

In Blandford Forum, Mr Warren declared that he had not
quite retired the fleet. 'In the newspapers they said it was the
last time, but there will be a few more. Not many.' He finds
the travelling more of a chore, and when you finally arrive it
can take four or five hours to set up. His eyesight is failing
a bit, he said, which is making the painting difficult, but at
least his hands remain steady. The models are fragile; he made
all the wooden boxes his ships travel in. 'All 252 that we took
down fit into my Focus estate,' he told me. 'I haven't got a
shed. I live with my son and daughter-in-law, and we managed
to find a house with an annexe for me, because sadly I lost
my wife a few years ago now.'

I wondered what would happen to the fleet when he too
passed away. 'I have no idea. I would love them to go into
some museum somewhere or other. But it's a very expensive
game. They can't be shown like I show them now on open
tables. We have to think about humidity and temperature
and everything else. And most museums are strapped for
space and cash. It's going to be a tricky one.' But there may
yet be a solution from within the fold. 'When he was helping
me lay out the display, my son said to me, "You know, Dad,
I'd quite like to do this myself later on." From my point of
view that would obviously be the best result of all. Because

he's grown up with them he knows how to pack them and he's become quite good in identifying which one goes where.'

The more I talked to Mr Warren, the more I envied his life, or at least his pastime. He had, after all, the sort of hobby that really was a hobby, a devotion that spoke of an ordered and sheltered life, if a detached one. He seemed to have his priorities both right and wrong at the same time. To maintain a miniature hobby through all those years – was that a sign of solidity or blockage? Was it maladjustment or high practical achievement? Mr Warren spoke of it as pure pleasure.

The pleasure was in the viewing too. It is not a passion bordering on chaos, of the sort Walter Benjamin believed afflicted all obsessives. Rather, it is ordered and sensible. His impressive, virtuous and repetitive display (the wonder of it is the wonder of it), brought to mind the French film *Le Dîner de cons*, a caper in which smug wealthy professionals are encouraged to bring an idiot to dinner. The idiot will entertain them, and, in bald Shakespearean fashion, reveal the other guests to be the fools they really are. Made in 1998, *Le Dîner de cons* was both a critical and commercial hit, and inspired many remakes in various languages, including the Hollywood retread with Steve Carell called *Dinner for Schmucks*. In this version, the schmuck constructs mouse dioramas (or 'mouseterpieces'), in which stuffed mice are all costumed protagonists from history – the rodent as miniature Mona Lisa, Benjamin Franklin, Wellington and Napoleon. In the original French version, the idiot is also a modeller,

but a traditional one, making intricately scaled-down repro-
ductions of famous landmarks. He makes unsinkable wooden
ships, he builds a small grounded Concorde, and – *mais oui*
– he makes a 346,422-matchstick reproduction of the Eiffel
Tower. His dinner guests scoff that his work is pointless, but
he's happier in his world than they may ever be in theirs.

'The domain of neurotic men living in attics': Ronald McDonald gets the Chapman Brothers treatment.

Mini-break, 2016:
London's Artists

'Basically there'll be lots of very unhappy people sliding down here,' Dinos Chapman said, 'getting cut by the nasty rusty edges . . . and a big pile of them here all crying, and obviously all going up for second helpings, because in hell no one dies, it just keeps going, over and over and over.'

The model he referred to was made the old way, from wood and resin and glue. It was a helter-skelter, rickety and charcoal-coloured, something from a horror movie scene in a playground with a dark sky perhaps, or a concentration camp, and it was sited within a walled box that would soon be encased in a vitrine. Nine of these vitrines would be mounted on a platform of stilts, and will fill a room, and be arranged in the shape of a swastika. Ah, good old modern art! Dinos Chapman, a tall and bullish man at the best of times, with a gentleness in his voice that belies the horrors he describes, looked down upon the helter-skelter in his studio in Hackney. At its base were hundreds of deformed tiny corpses and limbs – mostly Nazis, but quite a few Ronald McDonald figures too. It was the Temple of War that H.G. Wells had warned us about. That, and the wilful corruption of the joy of miniature modelling.

Because of its familiarity, the Chapman Brothers' most arresting work – the gory pyres of evil, the depictions of industrialised genocide, the penises and vaginas on faces, a tiny Stephen Hawking in a wheelchair atop a cliff, even the large-scale purchase and gleeful defacement of etchings by Goya and watercolours by Adolf Hitler – doesn't shock quite the way it used to. Once you're known as a shock artist, people tend to fold their arms (Jake Chapman says that no one has ever actually admitted being shocked by their work the way they were once properly astounded by Carl Andre's bricks; they just assume other people must be). In the absence of shock there is sadistic humour and purposeful confrontation. One looks on with fearful eyes, but one does look.

The Chapmans' world view comes in three sizes – wall-size impressionistic etching and painting, life-size resin mannequin, and miniature – and the miniature works require an attention to detail that might be unnecessary (and might go unnoticed) in larger projects. Their tiny figures invite scrutiny and inspection, and their success is judged as much on accuracy and complexity as intention. For the Chapmans, the miniaturisation is a means to a consideration of banality, and the mass-produced industrialisation of human suffering. We tend to regard the scale of human destruction in Nazi concentration camps as colossal, but to the Nazis the scale may have been insignificant. Besides, the brothers say, their work is not about the Holocaust but revenge, for now it's the Nazis' turn on the ride. 'Putting something behind glass escalates the level of voyeurism,' they say, as the responsibility for the work partly switches from the artist to the viewer. The more minuscule the work, the more we enquire; we are implicated just by looking.

The models are made 'from various bits and pieces that you can buy, but there's a lot of modification on them', Dinos Chapman explains to a visiting BBC crew filming an episode of *What Do Artists Do All Day?*. They bought 60,000 toy soldiers and contorted them, disrupting their gentle role as playthings, the way children tend to do when boredom turns to experimentation. 'It gave us a sense of omnipotence to chop these toys up,' Jake Chapman says, noting that power over people – however tiny and however plastic – is still power.

The Chapmans' 'hellscapes' were not the first miniature thing to engage them. One of their earliest artistic collaborations to reach the public (in 1993) was called *Disasters of War*, which included a 3D rendering of scenes from Goya's etchings (1810–20) depicting the carnage resulting from Napoleon's invasion of Spain. The Chapmans' circular tabletop tableau resembles traditional toy figures on plastic mounds, albeit with scenes not found in the regular toy box: beheading, impaling, axing, nightmarish battling of giant birds, decapitation, swinging by the neck from posts, immolation, very unhappy babies, naked fleeing. Many of the figures were bought from hobby shops, then cut with a hot knife, bloodied up a bit, strung up with guitar strings, embedded in a base of polyester resin sprinkled with grit – eighty-three separate scenes in all, all on their own bases, the whole unnerving collection about 200cm in diameter, about the size of a queen-size bed, or one-three-thousand-five-hundredth as long as the Las Vegas Strip, 0.000000005 times as long as the distance from Earth to the Moon, or one-and-one-fifth the size of Napoleon.

Of course, something small can take ages, and may drive you insane. In 2003 the Chapmans made a chess set. It was typical of their work, except smaller: pink mannequins with lank hair on one side, brown mannequins with huge afros on the other. Obviously they had penises and holes for noses and mouths, the pawns were on one knee, and the kings and queens had people on their backs. It was intricate work, cute rather than shocking, apart from the shocking amount of time the set took to make. When asked whether he had learnt anything new from the project, Dinos Chapman said, 'Yes, not to do it again.'

But the chess set was merely a diversion from their latest hellscape. Surveying the latest model of damnation in his studio, Jake Chapman admits the ludicrousness of the task, and how the studio assistants employed to realise the brothers' work must be necessarily moved around from one role to another. Spending weeks painting the red and white stripes on the sleeves of 2,000 tiny Ronald McDonalds would send them screaming. 'If this work is about hell,' he says, 'it's not only about hell in terms of content. It's also about hell in terms of its hellishness in terms of production. It calls upon and utilises all sorts of skills and techniques which are by themselves worthless, and not associated with the idea of making avant-garde cutting-edge art. This is the domain of neurotic men living in attics.'

Famously, and fittingly for a vision of fiery damnation, their miniature version of torment was burnt in a warehouse fire in 2004. The inferno consumed the entire contents of the art storage facility Momart in the East End of London, including many pieces by Damien Hirst, Tracey Emin, Chris Ofili and Patrick Heron. The Chapmans, publicly more amused than saddened by the fire, swiftly resolved to recreate what they could, and not just their own work: always interested in the processes of appropriation and mass production, and the suggestion that originality in art is neither possible nor terribly desirable, they believed they could reproduce the work of other artists too. They stopped just after their re-stitching and re-erection of Tracey Emin's tent *Everyone I Have Ever Slept With*, agreeing it was too much of a pointless faff. But the Chapmans did rebuild their vision of hell, which, in an expanded and improved form, they called *Fucking Hell*. And then *Fucking Hell* (from 2008) was elaborated upon in another nine-vitrine creation called *The End of Fun* (2010), which featured Ronald McDonald canoeing with sharks, and several figures of Adolf Hitler painting at an easel. Then there was *The Sum of All Evil* (2012–13), more McDonalds and Nazis, but also more dinosaurs, zombies and skeletons. And then *To Live and Think Like Pigs* (2017), the same but more extreme, if that's possible. We may never be rid of them.

Jake Chapman maintains that darker pessimism and relentless nihilism is all they may logically offer at any scale. Their miniature hellscapes and their Goya enhancements are never-ending, the brothers say, both their greatest hits and their greatest millstones. Dinos Chapman in particular talks of it as a chore, but something that as artists they are fated to do. In all the hellscapes, the Nazis are being recycled within their own mechanism of genocide, an endless helter-skelter, a self-generating volcano in continual spew. The impression – because of their scale, because of our presence above them, peering over – that we may somehow intervene in these vile circuses only increases their power. No other modern artist has used the miniature form to such provocative effect, although many have adopted a more contemplative approach. In 2013, Ai WeiWei reduced his experience of his eighty-one-day detention in a Chinese prison to a series of six half-scale fibreglass dioramas suggesting both the mundanity and inhumanity of his interrogation (he shows himself under constant guard, even while sleeping). His aim, he said, was to exorcise a terrible experience, and to explain his circumstance to as wide an audience as possible. By encasing the dioramas in large iron boxes, his cell resembles a room in a doll's house; the viewer adopts the role of a guard, checking up.

Rachel Whiteread's haunting *Place (Village)*, on permanent display at the V & A Museum of Childhood, is an assemblage of about 150 mismatched doll's houses piled upon two hills of tea chests and fruit crates. Whiteread collected the houses over a period of twenty years, and says she finds them fascinating as repositories of memory and family history. The houses are lit from inside but are apparently unoccupied, lending an air of melancholy and unease. The viewer creates their own narrative; there are more questions than answers.

Under constant watch: Ai WeiWei in a steel-lined box at the
Royal Academy.

There is just one further question for the Chapmans: Why
so many tiny Ronald McDonalds? McDonald's – the restaurants, the burgers, the Hamburglar and Ronald – features in
a lot of their hellscapes. There's *Arbeit McFries* (2001), a
stand-alone work spotlit at Tate Britain, perhaps the best and
worst pun in modern art this century, an exploded burnt-out
shell of a restaurant with birds of prey on the roof (all made
– should we need reminding of this – from model figures,
wood, metal, resin, plastic and paint). And then there's Ronald

crucified above a sea of skulls, Ronald balancing on decrepit playground apparatus, the burger joint in a caveman setting with a Flintstones car, the Golden Arches made from tusks, the McDonald's name written in bones.

For Jake Chapman, the fast-food chain is a useful benchmark for modern society in a diseased state beyond redemption. 'We take McDonald's as being a marker of the transformation from industrialisation to the end of the world.' (Jimmy Cauty's model *The Aftermath Dislocation Principle*, which we encountered in Chapter 2, is similarly littered with McDonald's iconography.) Chapman once enjoyed the idea of the company providing cheap fuel for the masses, an egalitarian facility. His model now represented the depletion of the ozone layer and 'a litigious clown who's lost his sense of humour'.

In what would seem to be a natural progression, the brothers have also made a series called 'Unhappy Meals'. These take regular Happy Meals boxes and etch the hell out of them, with lots of grotesque figures where pleasant green valleys ought to be, images of teddy bears and Ronald with his entrails splurging – just your everyday angry boy fantasy. Inside the box there is no food, and certainly no toy (the toys are already upending Nazis).

The Chapmans are not the only saboteurs to subvert the relationship between play and pleasure, nor between toys and the Third Reich. In 1995 the Polish artist Zbigniew Libera wrote to Lego for some bricks for an unspecific new project he was working on. Lego kindly obliged, and so when the resulting work appeared in public a year later the artist could legitimately, if disingenuously, claim that it was 'sponsored by Lego'. Lego was not hugely pleased, because Libera had used their gift to construct a concentration camp.

Libera used some original pieces as they came, and doctored others. Commandants had been assembled from pirates, a police station became a camp barracks, and a garage a torture chamber. Everything was clean, clinical and unbearably polite, but the civility hid terrible truths. Because of the nature of Lego bricks and figures, and our overwhelmingly pleasant memory of them from childhood, the sight of tiny skeletons being marched towards their deaths by a tiny armed guard is doubly chilling (the camp is surrounded by wire; another guard barks instructions from an observation tower). As with the crime models of Frances Glessner Lee, we are encouraged to examine the horror at close quarters, and to identify with a terrible plight. But we can't help but marvel at the snappy artistry too, the exploitation for gainful amusement.

The artwork came in seven boxes, with the camp ready for assembly inside. There was a faint suggestion – from those who chose to defend Libera from Lego lawyers and members of the outraged public – that the pieces could be made into anything the assembler wished, with the camp only one option out of thousands, but they weren't fooling anyone. An image of what the finished model should look like was on the box: a room to apply electrodes to a prisoner's brain; a fateful 'shower' block. (Long gone are the days when a child, buying a box of plastic bricks, would be clueless as to what to make with them, for Lego had long since traded its suggestive powers of imagination for a close alignment with the entertainment industry. You bought a box of Lego with a *Guardians of the Galaxy* Abilisk spaceship on it, and there was no point making a lesser spaceship or a car. And the same applied to a concentration camp.)

Lego tried to sue, but public and media support for Libera's artistic integrity encouraged the company to drop the case. The boxes were bought by the Jewish Museum in New York, and displayed in 2002 alongside something hellish from the Chapman Brothers. It was suggested that the models may encourage viewers to think of atrocity in a new light: by reducing the ordeal to the size of a toy the horror would not be lessened but heightened, the banality of evil scrutinised in a manner that made it both digestible and incomprehensible. Or comprehensible, given the scale.

'Excitement and heart bubbling joy': Sir Laurence Olivier with Denys Lasdun's National Theatre in 1967.

Chapter Nine

Theatre of Dreams

There is a photograph, taken in the mid-'60s, of what looks to be a rubbish tip, but is in fact a pile of discarded models for London's National Theatre. The photo shows a large tumbling pile of balsa wood and cardboard, and in the pile one can discern a few semicircular models of raked seating, and a few cross-sectional boxes, but mostly it's just layers of scraps and offcuts. The photograph speaks of endless hours and spent energy, and, if one knows the full saga of the National Theatre's tortuous gestation, of British conservatism and disdain. But after years of compromise and negotiation, a great building did rise.

The building was the work of Denys Lasdun, and the models the work of Philip Wood. Though Lasdun took much of the praise (and flak) for the brutalist monument that appeared next to the Royal Festival Hall on London's South Bank, he was in no doubt that it was the brilliant three-dimensional visual aids of his chief model maker that enabled such a striking building to be approved and then built. Sir Laurence Olivier, one of the most outspoken members of the National Theatre's board and the theatre's first artistic director, was not the sort of man to comprehend the quasi-academic descriptions of interlocking split-level abstractionist aesthetics, but a scaled impression in balsa wood was a different matter. 'Sleep I could not,' Olivier wrote in a letter to Lasdun in 1965, 'for excitement and heart bubbling joy at what you had shown us in that marvellous model. Oh my God if the government don't – not only pass, but promulgate and *extol* the enterprise now, I think I shall give up everything and go and eat bananas in Pitcairn Island.'

In the prolonged consultation period that accompanied Olivier's rapture, light was shone through the model, sections were lifted out and taken apart, and it was endlessly revolved. The model's staircases and railings were scrutinised to the last rivet. A significant section that was planned for an adjoining opera house was removed, and the location of the theatre building was changed, transforming its presence over the Thames and upon the skyline – the impact of both clearly visible with the model. The theatre's three performance spaces – the amphitheatre spread of the Olivier Theatre, the proscenium arch of the Lyttelton Theatre, and the flexible possibilities of the Cottesloe (now the Dorfman) – were scrupulously examined from all angles (a feat still possible today: a final-build model has been proudly Perspexed at RIBA's London headquarters in Portland Place). The National Theatre opened in 1976, and the initial public astonishment at the building all but overshadowed the performances within.

* * *

Andrew Garfield, Nathan Lane and Denise Gough are in the wings at the Lyttelton. It is Thursday, 4 May 2017, the press night of *Angels in America* by Tony Kushner, one of the great plays of the twentieth century. The question is, will it also be regarded as one of the great plays of the twenty-first century?

After an opening monologue, the stage opens on Nathan Lane playing Roy Cohn, an egomaniacal New York lawyer (he's on the phone, bullying his way through several calls; he sees the universe as a sandstorm of splintered glass). The next scene has Denise Gough as Harper Pitt, a Mormon out of her mind with loneliness and Valium ('Everywhere,' she says, 'things are collapsing, lies surfacing, systems of defence giving way.'). And this is followed by the scene where Andrew Garfield (Prior Walter) reveals to his lover a cancerous purple blotch on his arm, a symptom of HIV ('I'm a Lesionnaire . . . my troubles are lesion.'). This is all in the first twenty minutes or so, after which the play never lets up, and in the course of two parts and almost eight hours, takes the audience to Manhattan, Antarctica, Brooklyn, Salt Lake City, several apartments, several offices, a bar and a restaurant and hospital wards, and, ultimately, Heaven. In the course of sixty scenes there are real worlds and dream worlds, and ghosts and apparitions, and it all happens in real time. How is this possible? Great acting, of course, and great direction. And then there is the work of Ian MacNeil.

A few weeks after the play opened to outstanding reviews, MacNeil was in a small room at the National explaining how, about fourteen months before, the characters were about 2 inches high within a scale model the shape of a large hatbox.

The standard figures within it have nothing to do with America in the 1980s, when the play is set. Instead they resemble classic characters from a Restoration comedy – big wigs and foppish. But there is also one thinner, greyer, more modern figure in what appears to be a long, beautifully cut coat. 'I always use him,' MacNeil says, 'a slight architectural abstraction of a man. American, I think.'

MacNeil, who is in his late fifties, is an experienced and highly accomplished theatre designer (or 'scenic' designer, as he's described in the United States), and he's something of a purist. His credits include extensive work at the Royal Court, the West End and several shows on Broadway, where he won a Tony Award for his staging of *Billy Elliot: The Musical* and a Drama Desk Award for *An Inspector Calls*. But designing *Angels in America* presented so many problems of complexity and audience engagement that he began to wonder, in a manner familiar to all creative talents, whether this was the show where he'd be found out. 'Only by thinking the whole production could fall apart might it cohere and work,' he said. 'It's the same reason actors throw up before they go on stage – it's thinking they may be terrible that makes them great.'

Designers are responsible for rhythm, both in movement and timing. They're also responsible for an audience's point of view, directing the visual focus and close-up the way a painter may direct one's eye over a canvas. 'I think there's a misunderstanding about what designers really do,' MacNeil says. 'Theatre is continuous, and in this case it's a very long play. The responsibility of having someone sat in one place for seven and a half hours is huge, and frankly, words alone are not going to get you through it, not in the Lyttelton. Half of it is brilliant poetry, but it has to be a narrative event.'

At the beginning of his challenge, MacNeil had only the playwright's own words for guidance. 'The play benefits from a pared-down style of presentation, with minimal scenery and scene shifts done rapidly (no blackouts!),' Tony Kushner writes at the start of his text. 'The moments of magic . . . are to be fully realized, as bits of wonderful *theatrical* illusion – which means it's OK if the wires show, and maybe it's good that they do, but the magic should at the same time be thoroughly amazing.' The magic he describes includes a book that suddenly bursts into flames, a ladder ascending to Heaven, and the very physical appearance of the angel. With the exception of one cataclysmic blackout, MacNeil and the director Marianne Elliott made an early decision to honour every stage direction in Kushner's original text.

To begin, he brought it down to miniature. As always, MacNeil began with sketches on paper, but soon afterwards he and his assistant Jim Gaffney reverted to another format to better interpret and explain their ideas: a traditional scale model box within which they would establish their principal architecture, both real and imaginary. The box, MacNeil explains as he raises and drops thin card inserts at various depths, is not unlike a home-made puppet theatre. It is now, in his summation, 'knackered', the result of much experimentation and demonstration. It was this box that MacNeil presented to help explain both his grand visions for the play, and his detailed solutions to the play's particular dilemmas.

MacNeil was attracted to the delirious and baroque nature of the play, something that reminded him of grand opera. He had seen a sparing production Ivo van Hove had directed in Amsterdam, in which the stage appeared largely bare, and a record player played Bowie songs, and this freed him up to consider going for full-on glare again, at least some of the time. The opening scenes would all happen downstage near the audience with traditional scenery and props, and then, once the hallucinatory properties of the play began to take hold, they would give way to the open spaces of the stage behind. MacNeil calls it the 'pretend minimalist actually maximalist' production, 'the thing that wallops you with scenery and then takes it all away'. Classically, MacNeil went small in order to leave the biggest and most memorable impression as the audience departed.

The model box reveals that the actors are initially bound together by three concentric revolving circles. Before the circles dissolve to the side and back of the stage, revealing the vast expanse behind that will serve, among other things, as both a region and a distant Salt Lake City, the characters within the three circles invade each others' spaces – a literal Venn diagram. A short while later, an additional surprise: a new narrow promontory rises at the very front of the stage to represent a hospital room and a domestic apartment. There are two more surprises to come: a separate dreamlike world framed by neon, which gives the play a different visual rhythm; and a vast suspended piece of filigree metal studded with lights and suspended from the ceiling. This piece has been nicknamed the Lobster. 'I learnt that if you're going to do something big and difficult and unwieldy and expensive that makes everyone grumpy,' MacNeil says, 'you have to bring it down to scale and call it a cute name. It's the only way they'll give it to you, if you and they are affectionate about it.' (The 'they' are all the obstacles within MacNeil's field of vision, not least the production budget and set builders.)

He showed Tony Kushner the model over Skype and remembers being nervous. 'Writers aren't necessarily great with visuals,' he says. 'And there's also a great leap from modelling a box to dealing with a large crowd of production people. We always begin by thinking the model box is the hard thing, but we're still in a fantasy with a model box – that's the pleasure of it, but also the false sense of security.'

I asked him whether there was a lot of compromise in the weeks and months after the model was presented. 'Oh God, yes. It's really really difficult. If you're an actor, and you have a bad rehearsal day, you can then go back in and do it better. But not with a model. It can be agony for me, because I don't do endless models. There's a gun to the head the moment when you have to produce the one they're going to build. I do it and then I stand next to it for the next few months biting my lip because I have better ideas.'

Despite his talent and his awards, MacNeil is little known beyond the world of theatre design, and that world's a small one. This is to be expected: most people who work with small boxes are content to remain within their own. One of the exceptions – and you'd be hard-pressed to name any others – is

Es Devlin, who is not only regarded as one of the most exciting and in-demand set designers in the world, but also the only one to have leapt the boundaries of theatre to work stunningly with Kanye West, U2, Beyoncé, the Metropolitan Opera, Luis Vuitton and the 2012 London Olympics, for which she designed the closing ceremony. She has conjured many more wonders too, often by playing with gigantic and minuscule scale (her concert set for Adele featured a giant eye, she made Miley Cyrus start her show on an enormous tongue; even when it's not strictly theatre, it's pure theatre). Almost everything begins in her office in London as a miniature representational box or sculpture made from card or resin, but Devlin is not so much in the stage business as the memory business. Her structures survive principally in the minds of the people who see her shows, where they may expand or recede, long after the models that first suggested them have broken and been piled in a heap.

Devlin spent seven years of her childhood in Rye, a medieval town in East Sussex, and the place had a lasting impact: Ry is the name of her first child. Rye is where Devlin first witnessed model making in the grand style, and where her visual imagination took hold. Near the centre of town, at the Rye Heritage Centre, is an exacting replica of Rye at 1:100 scale. 'The model tells stories that I was very captivated by,' she remembers. 'A ghost story or a fable, or a story of a butcher who killed a mare. I started to associate storytelling with models.' The house where she used to live is in the model, and when a Netflix documentary team came to see where she grew up, a special effect shrunk her into the model so that it looked like she was sitting on the gable of her roof. Her mind still wanders those model streets and houses, she says. She believes we may best perceive the history and workings of a city from an elevation. 'It's much easier to find a pattern if you're looking down on something,' she says.

At the beginning of March 2018, an ambitious new play by Matthew Lopez named *The Inheritance* received its world premiere at London's Young Vic. It examined three generations of gay men, and the responsibilities they passed on to their successors. The play had two forebears of its own: E.M. Forster's *Howard's End*, and *Angels in America*, and it shared with *Angels* an extensive running time spread over two evenings. The set was created by Bob Crowley, and it was directed by Stephen Daldry, who for many years was the partner of Ian MacNeil.

Towards the end of Part Two we are in Upstate New York. Vanessa Redgrave appears on stage for the first time, playing Margaret Avery, a woman who moved here when she learned that her son, who was dying of AIDS, was being cared for in the area. She shows another character around the house where her son died, explaining its history and significance. In the original script the house is a described as a full-size building, but in this first production the stage is almost entirely bare, and the house has become a delicately lit doll's house filled with imaginary ghosts. The model in the designer's studio has become a model on stage, and the effect moves many in the audience to tears.

'We would not be doing it with a crap merchandise product': collectable wares at the Vitra Campus.

Mini-break, 2017:
Germany's Tiny Chairs

If you're a design addict you may well be familiar with Design Addict, a website promising information on designers of furniture, lighting, dinnerware and accessories. You may also be aware of the website's vibrant readers' forum, which once in a while catches fire with white-hot debate. There are few things more amusing (or elitist or cross) than a riled designer. A few years ago the topic that caught their imagination, attracting seventy-seven fervid but often misspelled comments, was called 'Vitra Miniatures – Pretentious Crap?'.

It was based on the following premise: the furniture manufacturer Vitra, responsible for commissioning and making some of the twentieth century's great chairs (by Charles and Ray Eames, Werner Panton, Hans Wegner, all the mid-century modern masters), had decided in the 1990s to make scaled-down versions of its greatest hits. You couldn't perhaps afford the originals – the Marc Newson Lockheed Lounge chair from 1986 for instance, which went for auction in 2015 for almost £2.5m, or an original fibreglass Eames La Chaise from 1948, or one of those red and white Eero Aarnio 'Ball Chairs' you see in a lot of lairs in Bond movies – but you could possibly afford one at one-sixth of the size. Or perhaps not, as the miniatures themselves could also be rather expensive.

Contributor Number 1: Am i on my own here in thinking that they are a load of balls? I mean, who the hell buys these things? please tell me I'm not alone. I've seen prices for example of the classic eames lounge chair for £200!!!!! I mean ffs, who in there right mind would pay it?

Contributor 2: I actually collect the minatures but dont have the eames lounge chair, they are a brilliant thing to collect as I do not have enough space in my house to buy all the chairs I would like. What is the difference from £200 for a minature to £4,000–£5,000 for a full size one, could you not say the same for that?'

3: I think £5000 for a chair is equally ridiculous as £200 is for a miniture. I'm a huge fan of MCM (goes without saying being here) but can't agree with some of the pricing of certain design houses (Vitra being the obvious example). Anyone who pays £200 for something which is tant amount to dolls house furniture, frankly, IMO has more money than sense.

In 1953, the Swiss shopfitter Willi Fehlbaum was on holiday in New York City when his taxi passed a shop with an Eames chair in the window. Liking it very much, he struck a deal with the manufacturer Herman Miller to produce the chair in Europe. Where should it be made? On a flat scrap of land inherited by his wife Erika in the most south-westerly part of Germany known as Weil am Rhein, which was not, even with a nice flowering of cherry trees each spring, a very elegant city (it was twinned with the far more elegant Bognor Regis). But here Vitra manufacturing was born, and the Fehlbaums became friends with Charles and Ray Eames and many other prominent designers who believed that a chair was not just a chair. Vitra (the name derives from vitrine) supplied offices and other commercial outlets, and a few products found their way into the sort of homes that appeared in influential magazines, after which they became ultra-desirable among graphic designers and other designers. And then, in 1981, just when things were going so well, and Vitra had expanded from chairs to all types of other furniture too, a lightning strike caused a fire that burnt down 60 per cent of the production site. The company had to start again.

The joy of starting again, if you have money, is that you can realise a vision. This is what happened with the new Vitra Campus, an attempt to celebrate design in all its far-flung forms, an adult playground where function met expressionism and the most daring and ego-crazed talents of the architecture world got to build stuff that few in their right mind would allow them to build elsewhere. What if, for instance, Zaha Hadid was to build a fire station?

The original plan for the campus (so called because it was

a place where the intellect could roam) was a modern but uniform look that would grow as demand dictated. One of the biggest high-tech names in the early '80s was Englishman architect Nicholas Grimshaw, who put up his first building on the site just a few months after the fire and his second two years later. The buildings were curved corrugated steel, functional and elegant still, set up to make the most popular chairs. But the plan for a uniform architectural look across the site was abandoned when Rolf Fehlbaum, the founders' son, had his head turned by a new friend.

Frank Gehry had built a reputation as a leading postmodernist before Fehlbaum asked him to design a building for the campus, which would also be his first in Europe. Two buildings in fact: a factory and a museum. Opened in 1989, the museum was a white confection of blocks and dramatic curves that appeared to be in continual motion, a building bursting out of itself. It was a direct precursor to the dynamism of Gehry's Guggenheim in Bilbao and Walt Disney Concert Hall in LA.

And because the Gehry buildings were so different from the Grimshaw buildings, the path at the campus was now set: henceforth every building on the site would have a daring look from an ambitious architect. Not all the structures would be new – a few of the smaller buildings, such as the Jean Prouvé petrol station, would be imported and then spruced up a bit – but all would add to the creation of cacophonous visual theatre. Today, a visitor may tour this twenty-five-year experiment and emerge with a feeling of confusion, exhaustion and delight, something like visiting the Pompidou Centre, MoMA and Tate Modern in one day.

In 1993, one building made the Vitra Campus famous. Zaha Hadid did indeed build the fire station, and it was the first major completed building of her career. It was commissioned specifically to house Vitra's own fire engines and prevent another calamity, but it soon became clear that Hadid was more interested in starting fires than quelling them. Fire protection was soon provided by a centralised service nearby, leaving the space free for art shows and receptions, and for everyone to admire Hadid's extraordinary work – the layers of sharply angled tilting concrete walls, the unusual vanishing points that make the structure look completely different from changing perspectives. Inside and out there was the dizzying sense that you were in a building designed by a maverick with something to prove. Students came from all over the world to pick their jaws up from the hard floor.

Thrilled as they were with the reaction to their project, the management team at Vitra were becoming increasingly concerned with their balance sheet; maintaining all these exciting structures, and hosting increasingly ambitious shows in the museum, was turning into a costly enterprise. And so, in the mid-1990s, a new revenue stream was hatched, and it was decided that their chairs should be made in miniature.

'We would not be doing it with a crap merchandise product,' Mateo Kries, the co-director of the museum, told me in his campus office in early 2017, 'but with a serious didactic object where you can learn something about things.'

Unlike the original chairs, which were designed for sitting on and gawping at, the miniatures were designed principally as an educational tool for students. Seeing the chairs at one-sixth of their size could transport the observer back to those fantastical moments when the design was first drawn up, and the Eameses thought it would be a great idea to make their plain moulded fibreglass seat into a rocking chair, and Harry Bertoia thought a chair made out of wire in the shape of a diamond might be something that would last. A miniature chair would make visible all the designer's frustrations with bending and bonding and stretching materials, and may inspire you to do the same. Suddenly, at the size of a paperback, it would all make sense.

Mateo Kries trained as an art historian and sociologist, and has been with Vitra for his entire professional life. He says that learning from small chairs inevitably comes at a price. At a reduction of 1:6, some technical details are harder to master than at full scale, which explains why the miniature van der Rohe Barcelona chair costs about £300, and a miniature beaten aluminium Newson Lockheed Lounge chair will cost more than £700.

'They are priced this way because we use the same material as the real chair,' Kries said, 'and it's not like a doll's house furniture where this doesn't matter. But very quickly we found there are problems: if you use the same thickness of leather in a big chair for a small one with the same texture it would look stupid, too thick, too structured. So we have to source new materials.' The same goes for the wood and the fibreglass and many screws, all of which must be lighter, tighter, finer.

Kries has a poster on his office wall showing the huge Vitra range, and it is impossible to examine it without selecting favourites. 'I'm asked that question very often and I'm never prepared to answer it,' he said. But today is an exception. 'This one is outstanding for me – the Rietveld aluminium [1942], just folded out of aluminium sheets, so ahead of its time. And this one, the Marcel Wanders Knotted Chair [1995], made out of carbon fibre and aramid, coated in epoxy resin and then dried as you dry your clothes, so you get a chair constructed by the hanging textile.' And perhaps a famous and popular one? 'I would pick out this one, the start of Eames furniture, the high-backed Organic Chair [1940] they did for a competition at the Museum of Modern Art in New York. There is a direct evolution you can trace from that first chair to so much of what came later.'

There were 224 chairs on Mateo Kries's poster, of which about 60 are available as miniatures in the shop next to his office. They begin with a garden chair made by Karl Friedrich Schinkel in 1820 and end, full circle, with the green Vegetal chair by Ronan and Erwan Bouroullec from 2008, and en route there will be historicism, art nouveau, Bauhaus and lots of experimentation with '60s plastic. The collection continues to grow, and soon chairs will come 3D printed.

Once you visit the Vitra shop, and place any of the sixty chairs in your palm, you may want to hold and buy them all, and nothing else, foregoing food. The chairs' initial purpose as an educational tool has long been superseded by their damn desirability. All the key elements of miniature collectability are intact: the chairs are exquisite objects in themselves; they are intensely and accurately detailed; they are limited in supply; and, because of their cost, not everyone can have them. They are also utterly useless – you can't employ them for anything, they have no intrinsic value (unless you swap them with the similarly smitten), and only the most masochistic would ever sit on them, especially the Gerrit Rietveld red and blue chair, which is all pointy elbows even at full size. When you do buy one, an instruction sheet confirms it is 'Suitable ONLY for decorative purposes'. When I asked Mateo Kries why the miniature chairs are so coveted by so many, his answer sounded like zombie sci-fi: 'You can't stop them!' he said.

Meanwhile, back at the forum, Contributor Number 4 reasons:

> What a rip! The first time i ever saw these little devils on ebay i thought they were the real thing and said to myself that chair looks like a good deal at that price, turns out it was a silly miniature.

> Contributor 5: That must indeed have been frustrating. I never understood those miniatures, when it loses its function (living, sitting, eating..) what is left? In a sense it is kind of degrading for the designer, who created the piece as a combination of several thoughts and principles, together forming an undivisible unity.

6: I think these amount to sculpture for some folks -- designers or architects in particulaur. This is what they dig looking at. Where is the pleasure in ridiculing someone for that? It's not that much removed from any other type of scale model when you think about it.

Now -- what I do find spooky and expensive and contemptible is when folks tattoo something, like say, the Eames Lounger, on their bodies.

7: I have not seen them all and I do not own any of them. But I share an office at the university with a colleague who has put half a dozen of them on his shelving. I must say that the quality is superb. Just enough detail to render the piece perfectly but not so much that it starts to look silly or doll's-house like. In some cases you actually wonder how they do it. Miniatures, from human beings to anything else on the planet have a innate attraction that might have to do with our tendency to control or dominate, or simply with the need for toys, I do not know? let's ask people that have earth globes in their interiors? but I am sure that most people will not be moved one way or another by rational arguments. This is all about emotions and god knows how much we are prepared to pay for emotions?

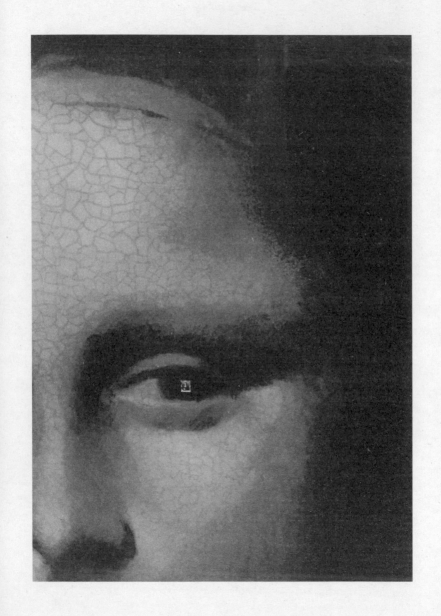

Chapter Ten

Our Miniature Selves

In the summer of 2017, at a small private gallery in Mayfair, I met a man named Willard Wigan. After shaking hands – his hands were large – he handed me a jeweller's eyeglass and led me to a familiar picture on the wall at the back of the gallery. The picture was the *Mona Lisa*, a good modern full-size copy by John Myatt. And there was something in her eye.

The eyeglass revealed that within her eye was another copy of the *Mona Lisa*. This measured less than a square millimetre, a mere speck, and, as far as the eye could perceive, was almost an exact copy of the original, including the frame. Trinity House Paintings, the company selling the double-Mona for £1m, issued a press release which claimed that Wigan's miniature was 'painted with the hair of a fly', but its creator told me otherwise. 'I used one of my eyelashes.'

Wigan, who is sixty, said he doesn't actually 'paint' his work, because all the colours would run; instead, he jabs. For the *Mona Lisa* he used not only an eyelash, but also oil applied to a fragment of nylon cable. As a cutting tool he often uses a shard of diamond he has smashed himself. 'It's manipulating, carving, cutting and scooping. For the *Mona Lisa* I made the outline of the frame first, and then had to make sure she fitted within it. I don't think Leonardo did it like that.' Wigan said that he always struggles with the thickness of the paint, and the proportion of the separate elements constructed over a period of ten weeks. Occasionally he found it necessary to file down the surface of his work, as when his subject's chest became too prominent in relation to her face. 'And I kept on having to push the mouth back.'

When one looked at the picture with the eyeglass, or when it was photographed with a macro lens, one could see that it resembled the original only in its crudest displays of colour and form; in fact, it was like the original picture had been constructed in jelly, all dabs and blobs. But to expect anything more would be to expect a mechanical likeness, something the micro-artist maintained was undesirable, if not downright pointless. He likes his work to reflect human frailty, not least the fallibility of human hands.

Pleasingly, Willard Wigan is from Wednesfield in Wolverhampton. He has retained his Black Country accent. He is sharply dressed in a grey suit with chi-chi crimson pocket square, and his open collar reveals a thick gold necklace. He has bags beneath his eyes like crescent moons. As befits his profession, he speaks with soft deliberation. His speciality is placing his sculptures on the head of a pin or within the eye of a needle. (This classifies him as a micro-miniaturist. The distinction between a miniaturist and a micro-miniaturist is exact: to appreciate the latter you need a microscope.) One of Wigan's most celebrated works within a needle is his interpretation of *The Last Supper*, with Jesus and his disciples all laid out and all recognisable from Michelangelo. He has also placed a row of camels in there, as well as the main characters from *Star Wars*, and Henry VIII with his six wives.

One views the work the way it was created – with a microscope – and each viewing elicits audible sighs of astonishment and delight. (One should be careful how one sighs, though: Wigan once breathed at the wrong moment while making his *Mad Hatter's Tea Party*, also in the eye of a needle, and found that, after several weeks of work, he had accidentally 'inhaled' Alice.)

Wigan said he holds his breath as he sculpts, but his claim that he 'works between heartbeats' is harder to fathom. Wigan told me he hated painting the *Mona Lisa* and doesn't much enjoy the rest of his work either. He made repeated references to ending up in a lunatic asylum. He said he enjoys the work when it's over, and the acclaim (and luxury lifestyle) it has brought him. He is used to people asking him, after the initial period of astonishment at his calling, precisely why and how he began this unusual pursuit. It started at school in unhappy circumstances.

'School was bad for me and I was always being humiliated. I had mild autism and couldn't express myself the way I wanted, and the teachers made me feel small. I felt like drilling a little hole in the ground and going there so that nobody could see me.' He said he often played truant. 'I hid in my garden, and I saw all these ants, and I got upset because I thought they were homeless because I had dug them up. I was five. I found a bit of razor blade and picked up pieces of wood and started constructing and building a house for them. Then I made furniture for ants and seesaws and swings.'

He remembered that when his mother saw his miniatures she was overwhelmed with disbelief. Apparently she then said, in a phrase that may be too good to be true, 'If you make them smaller, your name will get bigger.' (At this point, and at others in our time together, Wigan reminded me of a professional wrestler; not just the showmanship, which is an all-in pleasure, but also the hot air of the hype artist. His work was unbelievable to behold, and fragile too, and occasionally I wondered whether elements of his story weren't also a little far-fetched, or at the very least magnified.)

'I wanted to show the nothingness,' Wigan told me. 'I wanted to show people that we came from this molecular level, and how big nothing is. We disregard things we can't see. If you don't see something, it doesn't mean it doesn't exist. You can't see the wind.' Wigan moved from ant furniture to carving Beatrix Potter characters on toothpicks; he achieved good likenesses of Benjamin Bunny and Jemima Puddle-Duck. His big break came with the wedding of Prince Edward to Sophie Rhys-Jones in 1999. 'I carved both of them on a matchstick and called it *The Perfect Match*. The television companies were *very* interested.'

These days there are only a few things he won't design on commission. He has done the Statue of Liberty in a needle, Neil Armstrong on the Moon (in a needle), and the Obamas in a needle too. He depicted Cassius Clay fighting Sonny Liston in a boxing ring – on a pinhead. At the time I met him he was working on Richard III in full armour on a grain of sand. Not long after he had shown me the *Mona Lisa* in Mayfair, he removed from his pocket the Taj Mahal on a piece of Blu-Tack in a round plastic pot. The pot was about the size of a shirt button; the Taj Mahal was the size of a grain of rice.

Wigan said he thought the Eiffel Tower would be too hard for him because of all the metal cross-hatching, and he had failed in an attempt to sculpt a DNA double helix. His next big thing was a brand of watches into which he would place a unique object. The watch he was wearing when I met him contained a working Pianola. 'Don't underestimate the word "less",' he told me as I departed. 'Because my intention is to make people understand *more*.'

Willard Wigan claims to be his own inspiration, but he does have antecedents, and the most remarkable of these is a man named Hagop Sandaldjian. Sandaldjian was born in Egypt in 1931 and died in the United States in 1990, and between those dates and countries he lived a life of originality, fortitude and patience. He moved with his family to Armenia at the age of seventeen and became a skilled musician, specialising in the violin and the huge viola pomposa. One of his viola students introduced him to micro-sculpture and micro-painting (the student specialised in portraiture on grains of rice), and he immediately regarded it as a pastime that might improve his patience and precision as a musician. But it was only after he moved to the United States in the 1980s that he took up the hobby seriously, buying his own 125× microscope and gold and rubies to grind into dust; this he would then reconstruct as tiny figures on strands of hair plucked from paintbrushes and the sides of his own balding head. He sculpted a grandiose Napoleon on a pedestal, a golden crucifixion and Pope John Paul II holding a cross while delivering a benediction. But he was also fond of Disney, hoping perhaps for popular sales: he put Mickey, Donald and Goofy on a pinhead, but by far his most astonishing work shows Snow White and the Seven Dwarfs balanced along the side of a needle. All the characters show familiar bashful, dopey or grumpy traits. (Willard Wigan subsequently had the same idea, making the dwarfs smaller still.) Sandaldjian also carved sketches on rice, not least his own portrait, and he made a golden violin that measured 1/32nd of an inch. The violin had a broken neck, and the neck lay alongside it. He called the piece *Broken Dreams*, but as a counterpoint he also cut a message on a strand of hair that read, 'May all your dreams come true.' Sandaldjian would almost certainly have concurred with a theory advanced by the French philosopher Gaston Bachelard. 'The cleverer I am at miniaturising the world,' he wrote, 'the better I possess it.'

Photos show Sandaldjian as a dapper figure with a wide smile and broad sideburns, and markedly stubby hands. He established techniques that his successors would also come to favour: he worked predominantly at night, when the air was stiller and the rumbling traffic slowed; he tried to work between heartbeats. He sometimes played Bach over headphones to steady his nerves. Even then he reported many terrible losses of work through misadventure, which included breathing. His work could never be adequately secured under a lens for fear of crushing it, and so it often blew away; at first he would spend hours looking for it on table and carpet, but in the end he just gave up. He learnt to be philosophical about these losses, for no matter how wondrous and otherworldly they appeared to us, they could effectively be made again, and effectively made better (or smaller). 'An inventive spirit is what separates man from machine,' he once said. 'Man is the real technology.'

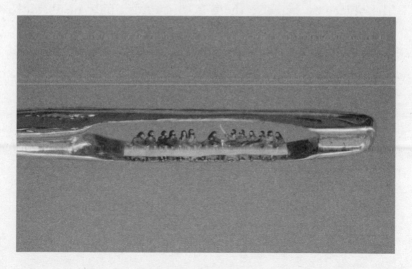

When Ralph Rugoff, the director of the Hayward Gallery in London, wrote about Hagop Sandaldjian's work in the mid-1990s, he was struck by the extent to which his micro-miniature world differed from the merely miniature. The miniature transports us to a world that is 'more precise and more brilliantly elucidated than our own', he believes, providing 'a shimmering ideal', a charming refuge from the failings of our ordinary experience. We do not just see smaller, of course, but better. Values become 'strangely enriched' at a small scale, and our outlook adopts 'concentrated power'.

But the micro-miniature, being nearly invisible, conjures 'a shadowless order of reality'. We are not only awed but bewildered, the way we could never be, say, by a model train set. Looking at Sandaldjian's work through a microscope, his creations appear to enter our own interior space, and 'the object we perceive there is so astonishingly insubstantial that we may be inclined to wonder where else it might exist but in our mental landscape'. By extension, Rugoff speculates, the micro-miniature enables us to anticipate other universes secreted within the world we already inhabit. 'Are there micro-symphonies to which we unwittingly remain deaf? Can there be truth in the musings of mystics who speculate that every atom comprises a universe unto itself, containing a thousand suns?' More practically, the micro-miniature may certainly lead us to considerations of our own newly fathomable make-up as human beings, and how everything is embedded in a strand of DNA. (Perhaps it's no surprise that Willard Wigan couldn't sculpt the double helix on a micro scale; it would have been like micro-sculpting the whole world.)

Thirty-three of Sandaldjian's micro-sculptures survive. He seems to have sold not one piece, and so all but one are in the collection of the Museum of Jurassic Technology in Los Angeles. The exception is a piece unfinished at the time of his death, a portrait of the eighteenth-century theologian Mekhitar of Sebaste, the inspiration for the Christian school Sandaldjian attended in Egypt. It is the smallest piece he ever attempted, and has been described by the museum as 'barely perceptible even when viewed through a microscope'. Which may make us wonder how small art can go without it endangering its existence, or indeed its usefulness. Miniaturisation for its own sake may be seen as a dubious pursuit: shouldn't it bring pleasure, or show us a larger truth, or in some way accessibly amuse? And should it not, at the very least, provide pleasure to its creator?

The American magazine *Nutshell News* was full of pleasures. It ceased trading in the mid-1990s, but for the previous twenty five years had provided its readers with monthly updates and gossip from the miniature world, and acted as a cheerleader in its editorials, inspiring its subscribers to ever greater heights of doll's house delight. In September 1984, for example, there was advice on how best to celebrate and miniaturise Bavarian Oktoberfest to a 1:12 scale. You would have needed glue, tweezers, cuticle scissors, ruler, paper, tape, toothpicks, X-acto knife, pencil, wax paper, brown and red Fimo modelling clay, wooden dowels, a coping saw, matte acrylic spray or fixative, and straight pins. Once gathered, you could make Black Forest cake ('cut 3/8" thick piece of dowel with coping saw'), red cabbage and dumplings ('roll small balls of Fimo, but don't bother about making balls smooth'), and sauerkraut and sausage ('mix three different shades of brown Fimo, starting with pure brown'). *Guten Appetit!*

Readers of *Nutshell News* were not children, but they were part of a larger family. Elsewhere in the magazine there was a letter admonishing the miniature community for losing its way. 'The world of miniatures . . . was made up of people working together, helping each other, and passing ideas back and forth,' wrote Tillie from Pico Rivera, California. But things had changed. 'As it progressed there emerged those who set themselves up in judgement on others, who didn't always reach out to help . . .' Tillie wanted things to change back again. 'This hobby is like a ray of sunshine – it should bring joy into our busy lives!'

Certainly the joyful world had turned commercial. One could make a Bavarian meal from a wooden dowel, but by the 1980s one could also buy almost everything ready-made. Bellevue Miniatures from Nashville had a basket of apples and peaches for $11, and Mother Anne's Birthday Cake for the same price. It's A Small World in Winnetka, Illinois, offered a tiny picnic basket with thermos, cups and saucers for $14. Cathy Anne's Miniatures, in North Hollywood, sold fruit cakes, muffins and tiered wedding cakes, with more than fifty designs to choose from.

Like the magazine that supported their trade, these suppliers have drifted away (or at least there is no trace of them online). But the digital age has not, as one might suppose, hastened the decline of miniature pursuits; in many ways it has enhanced them. Many of the online forum topics will be familiar – railways, ships, planes – and for any hobby there will be a thousand instructional videos. With no logical explanation, one of the great miniature digital obsessions concerns real and edible miniature food. A YouTube search for 'miniature cooking' produces 384,000 results, which is impressive enough, but the statistics for some individual videos in this number are ludicrous: in less than a year since it was posted, for example, a video of a person making a miniature egg burger with carrots and broccoli in Japan has been watched 16.6 million times.

These mega-watched videos, which presumably earn its creator mega-yen, are made by someone calling themselves Miniature Space. (Miniature Space also sells the same stoves and knives used in the videos, and they are popular: the stoves cost around $200, the knives $100, and several models are sold out; presumably, many are trying to make these meals at home.) Though based in Japan, Miniature Space's palate is varied and international, so we may learn how to make mini spaghetti carbonara (6.8m views), a stack of pancakes with syrup (11.4m), and 'Le Gâteau au Chocolat' *avec* icing (22.7m). The videos tend to last between three and ten minutes, and in general the shorter they are the more they're watched; some of us just don't have the patience for mini peeling and mini sauce reductions. That said, since Miniature Space lit its first mini stove in November 2014, its videos have clocked up 324 million views.

Is there a viable psychological explanation for this huge tiny culinary explosion? Or is it just miniature's ice-bucket challenge? The food itself is not remarkable and would garner minimal attention if made at regular size. Part of the fascination lies in the preparation. The fact that everything is reduced in scale – the chopping board, the *mise en place* array, the scales, the spatulas, the eating utensils, the colander and the cooker (with a tea light flame for heat), not to mention the cuts of raw ingredients – provides its own internal logic, which has always been a requisite in the miniature world. It appeals too because the hands one sees flip a coin-size omelette are anonymous; the food's the star, not the chef, which makes a nice change these days. And the hands show a love for the art, the true sign of the amateur. Plus, and above all, the food is tiny! Reactions in the comments section beneath the videos range all the way from 'wow!' to 'outrageous!'. One viewer, after watching 'Le Gâteau', writes *'Trop bien fait la cuisine en mode miniature'*, but the majority just say 'cute' a lot, or 'sooooo cuuuute' and 'soooooooooooooooo cuuuuuuuuuuuuuute!!!'.

You need beautiful nails and a steady hand to present well. But my lasting memory of these videos is not one of

dexterity and patience, or even how stupidly small the spoons look when held between the tips of two average-size fingers. The enduring impression is that the food looks so delicious. Try to sit through minibuncafe's ten-minute rendering of a pink carnation fondant wedding cake and not salivate, or not reach for something sweet. Or try to watch any of the miniature constructions of sweet and sour chicken and not think about ordering a takeaway. The only problem with these creations is that all their ingenuity may be devoured in one mouthful. The lamb in that rogan josh is finely cubed and slow-cooked with all those heady Kashmiri spices, and the rice is twice as spliced, but at meal time it barely fills a serving spoon.

There are other uses for a piece of broccoli. In the miniature world, broccoli may become a forest, and asparagus a row of tall trees, and an upturned mushroom a fishing boat. This at least is possible in the alert mind of Tatsuya Tanaka, a photographer from Kyushu, Japan. In 2011, Tanaka began posting new pictures online every day in a project named Miniature Calendar. You can still follow his work on Instagram, where you'd be joining over one million fellow followers in the pursuit of *mitate-e*, the craft of making small objects resemble something bigger and something else. But the master of miniature juxtaposition – art that not only makes you look twice but think twice about the concept of scale and the poetic poignancies it may offer – is a man named Slinkachu, who claims on his website that he has been consciously 'abandoning' miniatures since 2006.

The name Slinkachu may suggest a character from *Pokémon*, or perhaps a K-pop star from South Korea. In reality, Slinkachu is in his late thirties and was born in Devon, and his birth name is Stuart Pantoll, and those are the least interesting things about him. The most interesting thing is his work, which is consistently left to an unknown fate, including the whims of street cleaners and curious dogs, and the tread of shoes. Sometimes just a gust of wind may take them away. Slinkachu's work brings miniaturisation to the realms of guerrilla art. The best of it is both comical and affecting, and is frequently suggestive of society's ills. His figures are vulnerable not only because of their size, but because of their situations. Slinkachu's work regularly appears to be *true*, and elucidates the human condition, which is a rare achievement in work so small. How small? An inch or so.

When you see a piece of art by Slinkachu you will very rarely see an original; you'll see a photograph, for the original has long been lost to fate on city streets. (He works worldwide, and although he has sometimes been compared with Banksy, the main thing they have in common is the unpredictability of their locations. And like the work of Banksy, once Slinkachu's miniatures have been installed in these locations, it becomes impossible to imagine them anywhere else.) Slinkachu has published several collections of his work, and although the themes occasionally overlap – social dislocation, a quest for individuality in an homogenous world, the pursuit of pleasure in an atmosphere of threat – each photograph appears to carry a unique and deep backstory. A man sits forlornly on the rim of an adult-sized diamond engagement ring; the sad caption reads 'No'. A woman carrying her coat and bag walks alongside a crisp packet, her face determined; the caption reads, 'One day he will notice me'. Another woman confronts a pink sign on a metal post that reads, 'Fat? Lose milligrams TODAY!' A man in a grey raincoat stands atop a public payphone and gazes up at paper calling cards that read, 'Hot Dirty Tiny – Best in Model Village' and 'XXXtra Small' (yet another reads, 'Genuine Lilliputian, Pre-op').

We end where we began: at the Eiffel Tower. In one of Slinkachu's saddest photographs, a man stands with his hands on his hips selling souvenirs. He has four models of the tower available in various shades of silver and gold, each of them four times as big as he is. But business is not brisk, and he has made a small sign that reads '½ prix'. The photo was taken on a ledge in Paris, and behind the man and his trinkets looms the tower itself, out of focus but as grey and steely as it has ever been, looking like the tallest thing in the universe. The piece is called *Economies of Scale*, a pun and a disappointment and a modern predicament in one. Very quickly, looking at Slinkachu's work distorts one's whole perspective. Soon, the tiny becomes the norm and the merely small becomes enormous. In another image, a couple of boys prepare to hurl a Lego brick over a bridge onto the traffic below, and the brick, which is an eight-button regular, takes on the proportions of a house. In another, two children enter a play den, but the den is a standard-issue empty cigarette pack.

These are my interpretations of his work, and yours may differ. When I asked him about his beginnings, Slinkachu said that he thought it would just be interesting to leave little painted figures on the streets for people to find. At first, in 2006, he didn't even photograph them, but as he observed

the reactions of passers-by he realised there was a potential for a narrative too. 'Seeing the figures "lost" on the streets seemed to provoke an empathy in people,' he remembered. He believes that miniatures 'evoke this desire in people to rescue them and look after them, like we would want to do with babies or small animals. I still have many people ask me how I could possibly leave these poor little people on the street. I guess that if I can make people ask that question, if I can make them believe these plastic inanimate figures are actually alive, then I think an installation has done its job.'

Once he has a story to tell, Slinkachu's process involves

several steps. There is the use and amendment of standard German-made figures designed for railway layouts; there is the placement of these figures in the environment (a puddle, perhaps, or by the spikes of a metal fence), and then there is the photography, which often involves lying flat on the ground for the right perspective. Each of Slinkachu's stories is usually portrayed in two photographs – one close-up, the other contextual. The point of the story – be it a joke or a wretched social observation – is only revealed when the two images are examined together: a Bedouin with a camel on a desert sand dune turns out to be a Bedouin with a camel on a pile of builder's sand in the middle of a street in Doha, Qatar.

The titles of his works are usually poignantly at odds with the image. Small is rarely beautiful. A man has hanged himself on a thin branch of vibrant cherry blossom (*'Wonderful World'*). At other times a caption explains the image outright: a pink lollipop has fallen from a height to smash the windscreen of an Audi convertible, and the driver looks pissed off, and the caption says, 'Damn Kids'. In one image a father takes aim at a bee with a shotgun and tells his daughter behind him, 'They're not pets, Susan'.

'There is always a risk of the work descending to the realm of "cute",' Slinkachu told me, 'and I try to subvert or manipulate the audience's reaction to my work and miniature things in general.' There was also the risk, or perhaps the delight, that his work be used for fetishistic purposes. He has found his photographs posted on forums devoted to macrophilia or microphilia, the sexual proclivity for exceptionally huge or tiny people; in doing so, he reasons, people are playing with the traditional miniature pleasures of dominance and control.

'The challenge is to keep injecting meaning into my work and explore real human-sized issues,' Slinkachu said. 'I want people to see their own lives reflected in the figures, their fears and frustrations.' This is the real worth of Slinkachu's work: it is not the size of his figures, and it is not the juxtaposition of his figures in the landscape; rather, it is the emotions those figures encapsulate and explore. Like so much meaningful art, the miniature tells us a story about ourselves.

Wellington's smallest victory: the army assembles for William Siborne's
controversial model.

Epilogue: This Year's Model

This is the miniature's moment.

Jessie Burton's much-loved novel *The Miniaturist* is a best-seller and a BBC film. In March 2017, the most notable sale at the European Fine Art Fair in Maastricht is a late seventeenth-century Dutch doll's house containing 200 silver ornaments (the asking price was €1.75m). In January 2018, a nineteenth-century French porcelain doll sells in Maryland for $333,500, a world record for a doll at auction. At the cinema, the movie *Downsizing* features a 5-inch Matt Damon discovering that the dream life he was promised at Leisureland ('get small – live large!') is not all he hoped for. And the Lego movie franchise is now in its fourth incarnation: after *The Lego Movie*, *The Lego Batman Movie* and *The Lego Ninjago Movie*, we may soon expect *The Billion Brick Race*.

(The reason Lego hasn't featured more prominently in this book is because I've never been a fan. I distrust the ubiquity of it, the hard exactitude of it, the fact that it can emerge from a washing machine unharmed. You may feel differently, but to me playing with Lego is restrictive and stifling, as calculated as a computer game. I can't help but feel I'm part of a marketing strategy, which is not something one usually experiences in the world of miniature, and it doesn't make me feel warm and healthy, but compulsive and snappy. Almost all the miniature projects discussed in these pages display ingenuity and creativity in abundance, and they have been crafted from scratch, but with Lego one's creativity is carefully structured, and the challenge preordained, no matter how many brick-on-brick permutations there are. When my friend Johnny Davis visited the Lego HQ in Billund, Denmark, for the *Observer* in 2017, he found a company making 120 million bricks a day and a resurrection story to rival Apple, and also a company hell-bent on being the most powerful brand in the world – a tough thing to prove and quantify, one would think, but apparently Lego has recently achieved it, edging out Ferrari. 'Billund was built to function, not to please,' Davis was told by a Lego employee named Roar Trangbaek. 'There's not a lot of fun here.' And Roar was from the PR department.)

The central premise of this book has been that the miniature world reveals and illuminates a bigger one, so in lieu of Lego, here's one last short story. It shows the power of the miniature to reassess the historical record, and to proffer a new interpretation of something we already think we know.

In June 1815, fresh from victory at Waterloo, and with mud still caked on his boots, the Duke of Wellington wrote the first monumental account of the battle. The Iron Duke's simple narrative swiftly hardened into settled consensus, and his tireless self-promotion made his own account a difficult one to dispute. Everything happened so fast, and in so much smoke and blood, and with such a glorious outcome, that the public found it easy to bask in received celebrity wisdom. The generally accepted account went like this: in March 1815, Napoleon returns from exile to secure one final victory. Europe is mobilising against him, and so he decides to go on the offensive against Prussian and Anglo-Allied troops in the Netherlands, and on 18 June they meet at Waterloo. Wellington then adopts a defensive position, repels repeated French assaults and launches decisive counter-attacks. The Prussians provide a little support, but the brilliant tactics and mastery of the terrain are all Wellington's. The climax of Waterloo leaves 50,000 dead, Napoleon is exiled to Saint Helena, and British imperialism enters a new and commanding phase.

But then, in 1830, fifteen years after the battle, a military man named William Siborne set off to examine the truth about the final hours. He spent eight months walking the battlefields of Belgium and wrote to every living British officer who survived them. His findings, a ground-breaking example of forensic re-enactment, first appeared in his two-volume history of the war, and about a quarter of his study focused on just one day: Sunday, 18 June 1815. Almost two centuries later, Siborne's work is still regarded as a significant if controversial account, although his overwhelming analysis makes for chewy reading; in reducing the gigantic to the exact, pedantry frequently swamps narrative. Fortunately for us, Siborne also found a clearer way of telling his story: he created a model.

Like his written history, the model was both huge in scope and minute in detail, with tiny tin soldiers at work on many square metres of patchwork green. The model was 21 feet 4 inches long and 19 feet 9 inches wide, the scale about 9 feet to the mile. It took Siborne eight years to research and make it, and when it was first shown in London in 1838 all hell broke loose.

The model offered an entirely new interpretation of Waterloo. That Wellington outwitted Napoleon there was no doubt, but others who were present at the battle questioned the precise role the forces under his command played in the climactic hours. Could it have been the Prussian forces that ensured the final capitulation of the French as the evening of the 18th descended? Could William Siborne's model be Wellington's undoing?

Siborne, in his early thirties, was an administrative lieutenant with experience as a topographical draughtsman, and his earlier model of the Battle of Borodino had been praised both for its accuracy and its aesthetics. He was contacted by Sir Rowland Hill, the British army's commander-in-chief, and immediately accepted the offer of the new commission; it would be an honour to serve his country in this way, and it would provide some financial security. Wellington, who was then prime minister, was aware of the model's gestation and initially seemed to favour it. He saw no reason to have any influence over its construction, although this would be a decision he would come to regret.

The exactitude that was so evident in Siborne's written

account of the battle then extended to his model making. The model was built in Dublin, where Siborne was stationed as an assistant military secretary, at a cost of £3,000, equivalent to about £250,000 today. Siborne froze the action of the battle at about 7.30 p.m. on 18 June, the time at which the French Imperial Guard clashed with the British forces and their allies; if the model had been a modern war film, this is the moment at which the screen would fill with blood and flying limbs.

But Siborne's display was more pastoral than dramatic. The letters he received from serving officers provided details of troop formations, often accompanied by reports on the state of the crops in the fields and variations in ploughed or fallow land. Siborne explained that it was his duty as a craftsman and historian to weigh all the relevant information before placing each of his hand-painted tin soldiers on his turf.

The model was first seen by the public at the Egyptian Hall in Piccadilly in October 1838. About 100,000 people each paid a shilling to visit in its first year, and one may assume that many concurred with the glowing reviews. 'Nothing can be more perfect than the representation of the scene,' noted the *United Service Gazette*. 'Not only is every undulation of the ground most faithfully represented, but the position of every regiment, and its muskets and artillery are most beautifully and ingeniously indicated.'

The model may still be viewed today at the National Army Museum in Chelsea. Technically it is a wonderful thing, although today's visitor has to work quite hard to determine which forces are which and who may be in the ascendant. The model shows 70,000 soldiers, representing about 180,000 men from the actual battle; some are fallen. It was designed to be broken up into many small sections for transport, although given the amount of multimedia jazz that now accompanies it – a diorama overhead with smoke and gunshot and fallen men – it is unlikely to be going anywhere anytime soon.

One hovers over it as one might a post-game chessboard. A viewer may feel godlike in their aerial dominance of the scene, in awe at the minuscule detail and care that attends each figure. One can see why it took eight years to complete, and how, in the search for the precision that accompanies so much miniaturisation, the drama has all but disappeared. The task of interpretation is made easier by the addition of four touch-screen panels by which we may identify key areas and engagements.

Yet its frozen finality is deceptive. This is not quite the same model displayed in 1838, and it tells a decisively different story to the one Siborne originally intended. While the model was admired by those viewing the scene for the first time, the British who fought at Waterloo objected to the strong presence of General Blücher's Prussian forces, suggesting that Wellington had received far more support than he had mentioned in his dispatch; they claimed that the Duke's integrity and reputation were being tarnished by a powerful spread of fake grass and tin. And so, after the discrepancy surfaced, about 10,000 figures representing 25,000 Prussians were removed from the display, an absence that dramatically alters the military bearing. Today, the troops under Wellington's command have far more of a decisive presence than Captain Siborne initially believed they merited.

The case of the vanishing Prussians continues to be the cause of heated debate. Did someone get to Siborne? Would that someone have been Wellington? Did Siborne remove his Prussians after careful consideration of new historical evidence or with a promise of financial gain?

In the absence of conclusive evidence, the case remains unsolved. Siborne subsequently wrote that it had been his own decision to remove the Prussian soldiers after re-examining the facts. But this would seem to be an unlikely blunder for such a thorough historian and raises the possibility of a forced confession. Siborne was impoverished by the expense of his model, and he remained so at the time of his uncelebrated death in 1849. It is entirely possible that he modified his model to clear his debts.

There are other perspectives, and one of the most engaging is advanced by the Napoleonic expert Andrew Roberts. The aerial advantages assumed by taking an omniscient view of the action – a view we've seen throughout this book – was entirely absent from Waterloo. Yet a view from above was readily available to both sides in the conflict, and it could have won Napoleon the war.

The theory concerns balloons. Napoleon was aware of the military uses of the Montgolfier brothers' great invention: the news was everywhere in France in 1784 when Napoleon first arrived in Paris. A dedicated balloon corps had overseen enemy movements at the Battle of Fleurus in 1794, and messages had subsequently been carried by balloon as a faster alternative to the soldier on horseback. But the unit had since disbanded, primarily because the balloons so often caught fire. By the time of Waterloo, safety improvements had made aerial reconnaissance feasible again, and would have enabled Napoleon to detect that Blücher's Prussians had only been partially defeated by his men at an earlier battle at Ligny: he also would have seen their advance to Wavre two days before their vital contribution on the final day at Waterloo. For want of hot air and an aerial view – the ability, of course, to see the landscape in miniature – the future of Europe may have assumed dramatically different proportions.

Perhaps it has always been the miniature's moment.

The power and influence of the miniature in our lives has been constant and immense. Its ubiquity in the fields of art and architecture – the portrait on ivory, the maquette, the creative suggestions of minuscule figurines – has rendered great work possible. We've witnessed its impact in military and political circles, and we've seen how it may freeze a period of history at a scale of 1:12. But I think it's in the realm of domestic pleasure that we prize the miniature most. The ability to enhance a life by bringing order and illumination to an otherwise chaotic world – a world over which we may otherwise feel we have little control – cannot be overvalued. The fascination of holding in our hands something completely realised at an impossibly reduced scale is a wholly fulfilling one, and the satisfactions of inquisitive observation will never tire. At its simplest, the miniature shows us how to see, learn and appreciate more with less.

The movie *Downsizing* was a bit of a misfire, but it had its insights, and my favourite comes at the very end. The Vietnamese activist Ngoc Lan Tran, played by Hong Chau, is on a plane journey with Paul Safranek, played by Matt Damon. They are heading back to their tiny homes in Leisureland after a visit to a bunch of survivalist fruitcakes in Norway, and in her broken English Ngoc Lan Tran tries to sum up her – and our – adventures in miniature. She nails it. Her phrase is: 'You look around things more close.'

Not one to be outdone by a 5-inch Matt Damon, I decided to miniaturise myself. Once, this would have been impossible, or it would have required fantastic drugs, but the process is now common and legal, and at the end of 2017 I put down £199 to be photographed in a small white bell tent at Westfield shopping centre in Stratford, east London.

The tent was managed by a fifty-year-old sculptor from Glasgow named Jonathan Goslan. His pursuit was called Mini-You, an offshoot of the 3D printing company iMakr, and the promotional material offered to make me into an 8-inch 3D colour-infused sandstone composite. Before I entered the tent, Goslan explained that I would have to stand perfectly still as a vertical bank of fourteen cameras poking through holes in the canvas took 400 photographs from top to toe as I rotated slowly on a motorised platform (the apparatus was usually in the iMakr office in Clerkenwell Road, central London, but had been transported to Westfield to attract passing Christmas trade). I had brought along a small bronze model of the Eiffel Tower to hold as I spun around, but Goslan said that the detail would probably come out blurred, so he suggested Photoshopping in a tower during the production process and then printing that in 3D too, and it would look as if I had been holding it all the time.

I entered the tent. I put one hand in my pocket and the other empty palm-up at a right angle to my hip. Goslan said '3, 2, 1, freeze!' and the rotation and rapid snapping began. The whole thing lasted less than a minute, and when it was over I watched the layered images rendering on a display screen at the back of the tent. Once the photos had combined to reformat me back into a whole person, the 3D image would be sent to a 3D printer, and the result hand-painted.

I had my Mini-Me within a few weeks, and the first sight wasn't unnerving, as I had expected, but reassuring: it was a good likeness. It was a little like unboxing an Action Man, although I couldn't bend its arms or legs, and I wasn't quite so ripped. The model of the tower in the palm of my hand – about an inch tall – had come out perfectly. But then again I knew what to expect: I'd seen similar figures, and I'd been thinking about nothing but miniatures for a couple of years.

The reaction from those who saw it unprepared was different: they were astonished. There was surprise that such a thing was possible, and admiration for the detail. They commented on the accuracy of my hair, and the creases in my jacket and jeans.

'But why the Eiffel Tower?' some people asked.

Acknowledgements
and Further Reading

Thank you to everyone who helped me with this book.

As always, the whole team at Canongate has been creatively supportive and an immense pleasure to work with. In particular I would like to thank my editor Simon Thorogood, Andrea Joyce, Peter Adlington, Anna Frame, Lucy Zhou, Aa'Ishah Hawton, Jenny Fry, Vicki Rutherford, Allegra Le Fanu, Neal Price and of course Jamie Byng. And thank you to Jenny Todd and Jenny Lord, who got the whole thing rolling.

I am delighted to be working for the first time with Peter Borland and his illustrious colleagues at Atria Books.

My agent Rosemary Scoular, and Aoife Rice and Natalia Lucas at United Agents, have been unfailingly wise.

I always benefit tremendously from having Seán Costello as my copy editor.

My friend Andrew Bud read the manuscript before it was too late to change a couple of terrible misunderstandings, and thank God for that.

Four of the stories here (blotter art, Las Vegas, Zaha Hadid and Vitra) began life in a different form in the *Observer*, *Mail on Sunday* and *Esquire*, and I am grateful to my editors there: Allan Jenkins, Jane Ferguson, Simon Kelner and Johnny Davis.

The staff at the London Library have helped me locate much useful material.

A large number of people offered ideas and links to miniature worlds. Some of those ideas have been folded into these pages, but many alas have not, either for reasons of space, suitability, or because they were not especially good ideas. Many people reminded me to include the miniature Stonehenge in *This is Spinal Tap*, but I have nothing to say that could possibly improve on: www.youtube.com/watch?v=qAXzzHM8zLw.

I owe genuine gratitude to Catherine Kanter, Greg Brenman, Renée Knight, Tim Dunn, Heezar Norkus; Jasmine Dhiman and Theo Kotridis and their two miniatures; Plum and Andy Fraiser and their three miniatures; Hugh Mannzhou, Nicola Dunn, David Robson, Daniel Pick, Brad Auerbach, Andrew Marr, Naomi Frears, John Frears Hogg, Mark Osterfield, Andy Miller, Ben Garfield, Jake Garfield, Robert Dye, Richard Tomlinson and Stephen Byrne.

And my greatest thanks go to my wife Justine Kanter, to whom this book is dedicated with love.

I hope the following books and other sources will guide interested readers to new pursuits. But I should warn you that once you start with a model railway or making things from matchsticks, let alone seeing whether your acid tabs are still fresh, you may find half your life gone.

Bachelard, Gaston, *The Poetics of Space*, translated from the French by Maria Jolas (Beacon Press: Boston, Mass., 1994)

Benson, Arthur, *The Book of the Queen's Dolls' House* (Methuen: London, 1924)

Bondy, Louis W., *Miniature Books: Their History from the Beginnings to the Present Day* (Sheppard Press: London, 1981)

Botz, Corinne May, *The Nutshell Studies of Unexplained Death* (Monacelli Press: New York, 2004)

Bromer, Anne C. and Edison, Julian I., *Miniature Books: 4,000 Years of Tiny Treasures* (Abrams: New York, 2007)

Brown, Kenneth Douglas, *Factory of Dreams: A History of Meccano Ltd* (Crucible Books: Lancaster, 2007)

Calder, Barnabas, *Raw Concrete: The Beauty of Brutalism* (William Heinemann: London, 2016)

Chapman, Jake and Dinos, *Bad Art for Bad People* (Tate Publishing for Tate Liverpool, 2006)

Coombs, Katherine, *The Portrait Miniature in England* (V & A Publications: London, 1998)

Dillon, Patrick and Tilson, Jake, *Concrete Reality: Denys Lasdun and the National Theatre* (National Theatre Publishing: London, 2015)

Duffy, Stephen and Vogtherr, Christoph Martin, *Miniatures in the Wallace Collection* (Wallace Collection, Paul Holberton Publishing: London, 2010)

Elward, Robert, *On Collecting Miniatures, Enamels, and Jewellry* (Arnold: London, 1905)

Fritz, Morgan, *Miniaturization and Cosmopolitan Future History in the Fiction of H.G. Wells* (Science Fiction Studies, DePauw University, Indiana: 2010)

Furneaux, Robin, *William Wilberforce* (Regent College Publishing: London, 1974)

Garrard, Alec, *The Splendour of the Temple* (Candle Books: Oxford, 2000)

Goldhill, Simon, *The Temple of Jerusalem* (Harvard University Press: Cambridge, Mass., 2011)

Harriss, Joseph, *The Eiffel Tower: Symbol of an Age* (Paul Elek: London, 1976)

Hilliard, Nicholas, *A Treatise Concerning the Art of Limning Together With a More Compendious Discourse Concerning Ye Art of Limning by Edward Norgate* (Carcanet Press: Manchester, 1981)

Hofschröer, Peter, *Wellington's Smallest Victory* (Faber and Faber: London, 2004)

Hollander, Ron, *All Aboard! The Story of Joshua Lionel Cowen and His Lionel Train Company* (Workman Publishing: New York, 1981)

Hughes, Robert, *The Shock of the New* (Thames and Hudson: London, 1991)

Jaffe, Deborah, *The History of Toys* (Sutton Publishing: Gloucestershire, 2006)

Jay, Ricky, *Jay's Journal of Anomalies* (Farrar, Straus and Giroux: New York, 2001)

Jonnes, Jill, *Eiffel's Tower* (Viking: New York, 2009)

King, Eileen Constance, *The Collector's History of Dolls' Houses,*

Doll's House Dolls and Miniatures (Robert Hale: London, 1983)

Lambton, Lucinda, *The Queen's Dolls' House* (Royal Collection Trust: London, 2010)

Lasc, Anca I., 'A Museum of Souvenirs', *Journal of the History of Collections* vol. 28, no. 1 [2016]; pp. 57–71

Lévi-Strauss, Claude, *The Savage Mind* (University of Chicago Press: Chicago, 1973)

Lloyd, Stephen, *Richard Cosway* (Unicorn Publishing: London, 2005)

McNarry, Donald, *Ship Models in Miniature* (David & Charles: Newton Abbot, 1975)

McReavy, Anthony, *The Toy Story: The Life and Times of Inventor Frank Hornby* (Ebury Press: London, 2002)

Mack, John, *The Art of Small Things* (British Museum Press: London, 2007)

Miller, Daniel, *The Comfort of Things* (Polity Press: Cambridge, 2008)

Moon, Karen, *Modelling Messages: The Architect and the Model* (Monacelli Press: New York, 2005)

Morrison, Tessa, *Isaac Newton and the Temple of Solomon* (McFarland and Company: North Carolina, 2016)

O'Brien, Donough, *Miniatures in the XVIIIth and XIXth Centuries* (B.T. Batsford: London, 1951)

Oldfield, J.R., *Popular Politics and British Anti-Slavery* (Routledge: Oxford, 1998)

Reynolds, Graham, *English Portrait Miniatures* (Cambridge University Press: Cambridge, 1992)

Rugoff, Ralph, *The Eye of the Needle: The Unique World of Microminiatures of Hagop Sandaldjian* (Museum of Jurassic Technology: California, 1996)

Schwartz, Hillel, *The Culture of the Copy: Striking Likenesses, Unreasonable Facsimiles* (Zone Books: Brooklyn, 2014)

Sebald, W.G., *The Rings of Saturn* (Harvill Press: London, 1998)

Self, Will, *Grey Area and Other Stories* (Bloomsbury: London, 1994)

Siborne, Captain William, *History of the War in France and Belgium in 1815* (T&W Boone: London, 1841)

Slinkachu, *Little People in the City* (Boxtree: London, 2008)

Slinkachu, *The Global Model Village* (Boxtree: London, 2012)

Stewart, Susan, *On Longing: Narratives of the Miniature, the Gigantic, the Souvenir, the Collection* (Duke University Press: North Carolina, 1992)

Stewart-Wilson, Mary, *Queen Mary's Dolls' House* (Bodley Head: London, 1988)

Stott, Anne, *Wilberforce: Family and Friends* (Oxford University Press: Oxford, 2012)

Taylor, John H., *Egyptian Mummies* (British Museum Press: London, 2010)

Taylor, Joshua Charles (ed.), *Nineteenth-Century Theories of Art* (University of California Press: Berkeley, 1989)

Thorne, James Ward (Mrs), *Miniature Rooms* (Art Institute of Chicago: Chicago, 2004)

Van Danzig, Barry, *Who Won Waterloo? The Trial of Captain Siborne* (UPSO: East Sussex, 2006)

Wells, H.G., *Little Wars: A Game for Boys* (Frank Palmer: London, 1913)

Wells, Rachel, *Scale in Contemporary Sculpture: Enlargement, Miniaturisation and the Life-Size* (Ashgate Publishing: Farnham, Surrey, 2013)

Winslow, Colin, *The Handbook of Model-making for Set Designers* (The Crowood Press: Marlborough, 2008)

Winterstein, Irene, *The Irene Winterstein Collection of Important Miniature Books* (Christie's: London, 2000)

Wood, Marcus, *Blind Memory: Visual Representations of Slavery in England and America* (Routledge: Oxford, 2000)

Picture Credits

While every effort has been made to contact copyright-holders of illustrations, the author and publishers would be grateful for information about any illustrations where they have been unable to trace them, and would be glad to make amendments to further editions.

Princess Elizabeth visiting Bekonscot © Universal History Archive / UIG via Getty Images; workers painting the Eiffel Tower © Bettman / Getty Images; shabti © Shabti of Seti I / De Agostini Picture Library / G. Dagli Orti / Bridgeman Images; visitors to Bekonscot © Simon Garfield; Pendon plan © Pendon Museum Collection; 'Description of a Slave Ship', 1789 (print), English School (18th century) / Wilberforce House, Hull City Museums and Art Galleries, UK / Bridgeman Images; model of the slave ship 'Brookes' used by William Wilberforce (1759 –1833) in the House of Commons to demonstrate conditions on the middle passage, 18th century (wood) / Wilberforce House, Hull City Museums and Art Galleries, UK / Bridgeman Images; the Maria Fitzherbert Jewel (w/c on ivory in diamond-studded locket), British School (19th century) / Private Collection / Photo © Christie's Images / Bridgeman Images; H.G. Wells, 'Little Wars' © Illustrated London News Ltd / Mary Evans; Queen Mary's doll's house © Topical Press Agency / Getty Images; Frances Glessner Lee © Glessner House, Chicago, IL; Albert Einstein blotter art © Simon Garfield; Rod Stewart, photography by Hal Reynolds; Alec Garrard © Geoff Robinson Photography; Zaha Hadid © Christopher Pillitz / Getty Images; Las Vegas Strip © Ethan Miller / Getty Images; Philip Warren © BNPS.co.uk; 'The Sum of All Evil' © Anthony Wallace / AFP / Getty Images; AiWeiWei © Simon Garfield; National Theatre © Ron Case / Keystone / Getty Images; Vitra Museum © Simon Garfield; Mona Lisa © Simon Garfield; 'The Last Supper' by Willard Wigan MBE, as photographed by R.J. Baddeley. Copyright © R.J. Baddeley; 'Economies of Scale' © Slinkachu; model of the Battle of Waterloo © Royal Armouries

Index

References to images are in *italics*.

'Digressive, gossipy, thoughtful and thoroughly entertaining' *SUNDAY TIMES*

10

TIMEKEEPERS

11 59 60

12:00

HOW THE WORLD
BECAME OBSESSED WITH TIME

60
45 45
30 15 0 15 30

5

BESTSELLING AUTHOR OF *JUST MY TYPE*

SIMON GARFIELD

'Thoroughly enjoyable and illuminating'
Observer

CANON GATE

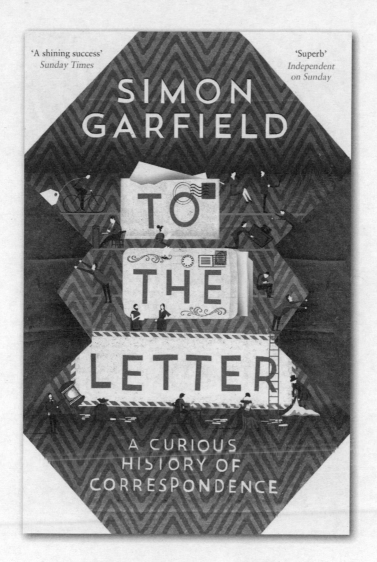

SIMON
GARFIELD

TO
THE
LETTER

A CURIOUS
HISTORY OF
CORRESPONDENCE

CANON⏸GATE

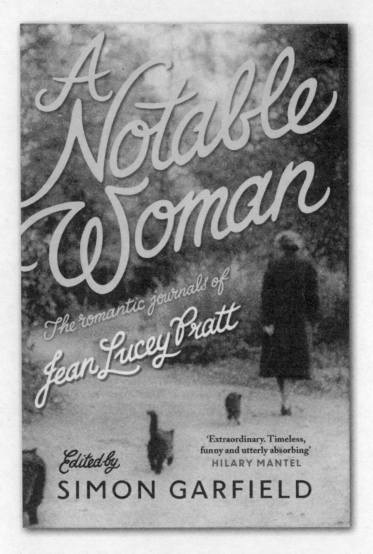

A Notable Woman

The romantic journals of

Jean Lucey Pratt

Edited by

SIMON GARFIELD

'Extraordinary. Timeless,
funny and utterly absorbing'
HILARY MANTEL

'Funny, tender and gripping'
New Statesman

CANON GATE